Great Map Mysteries

18 Stories and Maps to Build Geography and Map Skills

BY SUSAN JULIO

SCHOLASTIC
PROFESSIONAL BOOKS

NEW YORK • TORONTO • LONDON • AUCKLAND • SYDNEY

To Grandma and Grandpa Julio, with love

Cover design by Vincent Ceci and Jaime Lucero
Interior design by Solutions by Design, Inc.
Cover and Interior illustration by James Graham Hale

ISBN 0-590-89641-5
Copyright ©1997 by Susan Julio
12 10 9 8 7 6 5 4 3

TABLE OF CONTENTS

TO THE TEACHER

Great Map Mysteries is designed to help students learn the basic skills of map reading. People have been relying on maps of all kinds for thousands of years. Initially, they began as crude drawings scratched into the dirt by travelers hoping to share a simple knowledge of places and things with others. Later, maps helped people find food and water, places to live, and trade routes. Today, maps offer precise drawings of every place on earth. They can also provide important information such as weather conditions, time variations, and population densities.

Map reading can often be a confusing and mysterious process to children. I hope this book will help eliminate some of the mystery from maps and open new worlds of information in an interesting and fun way. *Great Map Mysteries* will help your students to find locations, and better understand several different kinds of maps. In time your class will come to appreciate how essential and enjoyable map reading skills can be for anyone interested in the world around them.

How to Use This Book

Great Map Mysteries can be used to introduce or reinforce different map skills. Lessons can be used in a traditional classroom setting or in a cooperative learning environment. Each map mystery includes the following: the case (a story that is built around a map skill), the Use the Clues section (a review of the clues given in the story and directions on how to use the clues to solve the mystery), reproducible maps and activity sheets, and The Solution (the answer to the mystery).

One way to present each lesson might be to begin by reading the mystery aloud to your class. Have students begin to think about the plot of the mystery and the clues. Then, distribute copies of the mystery along with the corresponding reproducible sheets. Discuss the Use the Clues section of the mystery. Ask these questions: What is the mystery? What clues can help you solve the mystery? What map skills do you need to know? Go over the map skills with the class to ensure understanding. Then, have your "map detectives" work alone or in groups to solve the mystery. When students are finished have them share their answers and demonstrate how they resolved the case. Finally, read The Solution to find out how Dectectives Hyde and Seek solved the mystery.

THE CASE OF THE
PUZZLING PRODUCER
Or Identifying Geographic Shapes

The Mystery

A sharp knock on the office door alerted Detectives Hyde and Seek to the possibility of a new client. Things had been a little slow lately. In walked a fashionably dressed young man wearing sunglasses. "Flick Gloss!" he announced reaching out and shaking the hand of each detective. "Got trouble. Big trouble!"

Hyde and Seek exchanged glances. "What kind of trouble?" Detective Seek asked.

Gloss stretched out in a chair and removed his sunglasses. "Ever hear of J.D. Smithereens?" he asked, chewing a piece of gum.

Hyde raised an eyebrow. "J.D. Smithereens, the big movie producer?"

Gloss nodded. "That's the guy. He's my uncle. I believe he's been kidnapped. You see, we were supposed to meet for dinner last night. I got a call from Uncle telling me he had to cancel. He sounded nervous and he didn't give me a reason. When I went to his house today, it was empty, except for this note."

Flick Gloss handed a folded note to the detectives. "If you want to see the big guy again, have $500,000 ready in a brown box. Wait for our next instructions. Do not contact the police or it's the end of J.D.," Hyde read aloud.

"Certainly seems like a ransom note," Seek remarked. "You really should contact the police."

Gloss blew a bubble. "Nothing doing, baby," he snapped. "We're talking family here. Someone nabbed him. Right in his own home. And I'll tell you something else," Gloss added, jabbing his finger at Hyde. "This was an inside job!"

"Why do you think that?" Hyde asked.

Gloss smiled. "Because only someone familiar with my uncle and his habits would know he always spends Wednesday nights with me. And there are no signs of struggle or forced entry!"

"I suppose it wouldn't hurt to take a look at the scene of the crime," Detective Seek sighed.

At the large home of J.D. Smithereens, Gloss lost no time in taking the detectives to J.D.'s study. "This is where I found the note," he explained, pointing to a huge desk. "I didn't touch a thing."

Hyde and Seek glanced around the large and expensively furnished room. On the desk sat a computer and an incomplete puzzle of the United States. A half-eaten peanut butter sandwich rested on a plate, along with an empty can of soda. Gloss looked sadly at the unfinished puzzle. "Puzzles—they were his hobby. Kind of dull, but go figure."

Hyde noticed that there were no loose puzzle pieces on the desk. "Seems as if he's missing five pieces," he murmured, scanning the floor. "Are you certain no one's been in this room since yesterday?"

Gloss nodded. "Positive. I've got the key."

Detective Seek folded her arms and leaned against the desk. "Did your uncle have any enemies that you know of?" she asked.

Gloss smirked. "Plenty! That old guy had more enemies than Dracula!" he said, narrowing his eyes. "Especially Strom von Drang, the script writer. He and Uncle almost came to blows the other night when Uncle refused to produce his new movie *Mud Suckers from Mars*. And don't forget that actor, Reels O'Film. He never forgave J.D. for not casting him in last year's blockbuster, *The Singing Coconuts*."

Gloss put his arm around Detective Hyde's shoulder. "Anyway, I want you to be the go-betweens. I'll get the money from Uncle's bank and you make the drop."

Detective Hyde looked up from the puzzle on the desk. "That won't be necessary," he said. "I already know who the kidnapper is."

"How?" Gloss shouted.

Hyde smiled. "Your uncle told me with this," he said, as he tapped the puzzle gently.

How?

Use the Clues

Hyde said the United States puzzle on J.D.'s desk helped him to figure out the name of the kidnapper. The detective noticed that the puzzle was almost complete, except for five missing pieces. Now look at the puzzle. Use an atlas to find out which states are missing. Then write down the names of the missing states. Together the first letter of each state spell out the name of the kidnapper. (Hint: You'll have to rearrange the letters!)

Name_____

What are the missing states?

1. _____

2. _____

3. _____

4. _____

5. _____

The kidnapper is:

_____

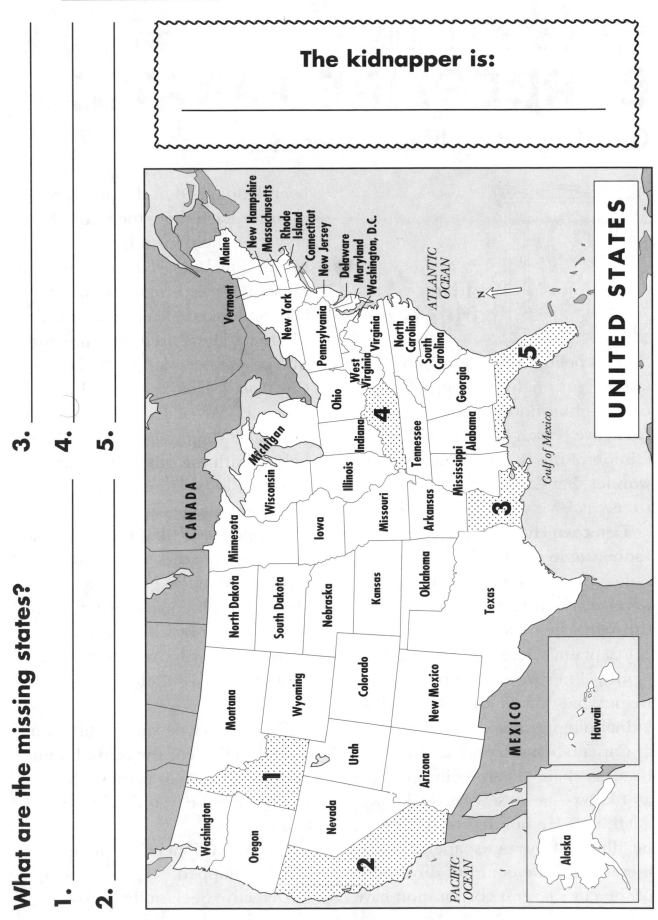

UNITED STATES

9

THE CASE OF THE
BORDERLINE FANATIC
Or Interpreting Map Borderlines

The Mystery

"I can't believe that a group of kidnappers might be operating in our neighborhood!" moaned Detective Seek, glancing at the latest edition of the Brown Times. "It's no wonder that Captain Schwab wants to see us!"

Detective Hyde nodded his head as the two went into the Brown City Police Department. Captain Schwab paced back and forth. "I'm through!" he moaned.

"Captain," Detective Seek said gently, "I'm sure we can be of some help. What do you know about this kidnapping business?"

Captain Schwab sank heavily into his desk chair. "I can easily tell you all I know—because I hardly know anything!" He pointed to the headlines in the newspaper. "Three members of the board of directors of the city's largest corporation have

been kidnapped in the past three months. Each time, the victim is abducted, held for ransom, and released in a deserted area once the ransom money is paid." Captain Schwab looked bleakly out of the window. "There are three directors who've not been kidnapped yet— Chi Woo, J. Hilary Cox, and Judy Coleman. We've assigned detectives to protect them, but that hasn't helped with the others. One of the three could be kidnapped at anytime! No one can tell us who the kidnappers are, what they look like, or even where they take their captives. All we've got is one slim clue. The kidnappers seem to speak to each other by whistling—you know—like birds. And, as far as I'm concerned, this whole case is for the birds."

Detective Hyde rubbed his chin thoughtfully. "For the birds, hmmm? Perhaps a visit to our friend Jay Finch might be in order," he announced.

"Who's Jay Finch?" Captain Schwab snapped.

Detective Seek smiled, "An

acquaintance of ours who owns the 'For the Birds' pet store downtown. If anyone knows what's going on, it's Jay."

Later that afternoon the detectives walked into Finch's store. Jay Finch was busily shoveling various brands of seed into plastic bags. "Hyde, Seek!" he grinned, looking up from his work. "Something I can help you with today? Suet cups, bird bath?"

Detective Seek shook her head and examined a parrot in a cage. "Know anything about the recent kidnappings?" she asked quietly. Jay's eyebrows shot up. "Why would I? I'm just a guy who loves birds!"

Detective Hyde patted his pocket. "Perhaps a reward might change your mind," he said.

Jay looked around nervously. "You think I'm a stool pigeon?"

"Better than being a jailbird!" Seek commented. "Come on, Finch, if you know something, talk."

"Well," Jay began quietly, "word on the street has it someone's going to be snatched tonight."

"Who!?" Hyde asked excitedly.

Jay put his finger to his lips. "Shhh! Quiet down! This kidnapping group has ears everywhere! Everyone in the neighborhood is being watched. But rumor has it that—"

Just at that moment the door opened and several men in dark suits and low-slung hats walked in. Finch turned pale instantly. "Ahh. . . as I was saying Mr. Piper, the birds you want to see, well they follow a special migration route. Here, let me show you." Finch took an atlas down from a shelf and turned to a map showing the states of Idaho and Washington. He winked conspiratorially at Hyde and grabbed a pen. "The birds start here in Moscow, Idaho, and cross the border to Spokane, Washington. From there they cross the border to Newport in the county of Pend Oreille. Then they take the big plunge across the border to the city of Trail in British Columbia. That's in Canada, see?"

Detective Hyde was in too much pain to see. Each time Finch had said the word "border" he had given Hyde a sharp kick in the shin. Anxiously glancing at the men in dark suits, Finch pushed the map into Hyde's hands. "Study that route and you'll find your man, ah, I mean bird. And here," Finch said, as he quickly put a small book into Seek's pocket. "This bird guide will identify what you're looking for. Happy watching!" With a slam of the door, he shoved Hyde and Seek into the street.

"Well!" Detective Seek exclaimed, straightening her skirt. "Finch was trying to tell us something. But what?"

Hyde thoughtfully studied the map. "And why did he keep kicking me whenever he said the word border?"

Detective Seek shrugged and fished the small book Finch gave her from her pocket. "How strange! This isn't a bird guide. It's a Morse code book," she said. Suddenly Hyde slapped the map. "Of course!" he shouted. "Migration routes, borders, Morse code!—the next victim's name is right on this map."

"Where?" exclaimed Seek.

Do you know?

~~~~~~~~~~~~~~~~~~~~~~~

Use the Clues

Hyde said that the map Finch gave him revealed the name of the next kidnapping victim. By looking at the migration route that Finch described he noticed the different borders the birds would cross to get to their homes. Borderlines are lines that separate pieces of land. Political borderlines divide counties, states, and countries. Look at the bird migration route that Finch traced. Then use the map key and Morse code to figure out the name of the next victim. Remember that Morse code is a system of dots and dashes that are used to send messages.

~~~~~~~~~~~~~~~~~~~~~~~

Morse Code

ALPHABET

A ·—	N —·
B —···	O ———
C —·—·	P ·——·
D —··	Q ——·—
E ·	R ·—·
F ··—·	S ···
G ——·	T —
H ····	U ··—
I ··	V ···—
J ·———	W ·——
K —·—	X —··—
L ·—··	Y —·——
M ——	Z ——··

NUMERALS

1	·————
2	··———
3	···——
4	····—
5	·····
6	—····
7	——···
8	———··
9	————·
0	—————

Name_____

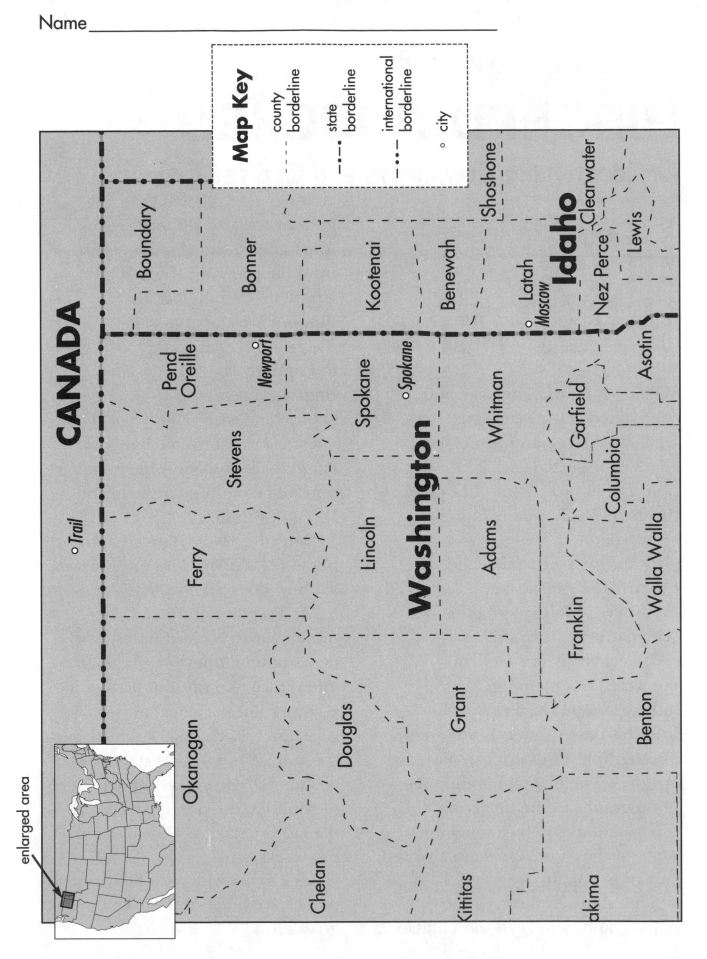

Map Key

- - - - county borderline

—··— state borderline

—···— international borderline

○ city

CANADA

Idaho

Boundary

Bonner

Kootenai

Benewah

Shoshone

Latah
○ Moscow

Nez Perce

Clearwater

Lewis

Pend Oreille

○ Newport

Spokane

○ Spokane

Whitman

Garfield

Asotin

○ Trail

Stevens

Ferry

Lincoln

Washington

Adams

Franklin

Columbia

Walla Walla

Okanogan

Douglas

Grant

Benton

Chelan

Kittitas

akima

enlarged area

THE CASE OF THE

PINCHED POOCHES

Or Identifying Continents and Capital Cities

The Mystery

William Pregoria, the official from the United Nations, greeted Detectives Hyde and Seek warmly. "Please, be seated," he said, pointing to two chairs. "I hope you can help. You've come highly recommended!"

Detective Seek smiled and sat down. "How can we help?" she asked.

Mr. Pregoria tugged at his beard. "Dognapping," he said.

Detective Hyde raised an eyebrow. "Dognapping?"

Pregoria pulled a manila file from his desk drawer. Inside were photographs of five dogs. "Not just any dogs," he began, handing the photographs to the detectives. "Special dogs. Dogs that belong to some of the most respected and well known people in the world."

Seek shuffled through the photographs and read the notations under each one aloud: "Teddy, American cocker spaniel, taken from the grounds of the White House in Washington, D.C.; Buttons, Welsh corgi, removed from the grounds of Buckingham Palace in London; Tue, Rhodesian ridgeback, removed from Cape Manuel in Dakar; Chu Nyo, chow chow, removed from Changdok Palace in Seoul; Nininha, poodle, removed from the Palace of the Dawn in Brasilia."

Detective Hyde glanced at the photos. "I see what you mean. Have all these dogs been stolen?" he asked.

Mr. Pregoria nodded. "The owners have received notes demanding money for the dogs' safe return. No ransom has been paid yet, but the dogs' owners are very upset. Each dog was taken very carefully. A new dog is stolen every two weeks!" He picked up a picture of Nininha, the poodle. "She was the last one taken. That was almost two weeks ago!"

Seek's eyes widened. "Then we don't have much time!" she groaned.

Hyde rubbed his chin thoughtfully. "You said that the dognappers must have a pattern," he said, looking down at the photos. "Let's get a world map and see if we can find out what that pattern is."

Mr. Pregoria provided the detectives with a map and a small box of pins. Carefully, Hyde and Seek marked each city where a dog had been stolen. All of a sudden, Hyde snapped his fingers. "That's it!" he shouted. "I know where the dognappers will strike next!"

Mr. Pregoria looked surprised. "That quickly?" he asked. "Where!?"

Can you tell him?

Use the Clues

By using a world map and some marking pins, Detective Hyde figured out the dognapper's pattern. How? Look at the world map. You'll notice that the earth is made up of bodies of water and large land masses, called continents. The seven continents are North America, South America, Africa, Europe, Asia, Antarctica, and Australia. Continents can be made up of only one country, such as Australia, or made up of many different countries, such as Africa. And one continent, Antarctica, has no countries at all!

Now, use an atlas to pinpoint the location of each of the stolen dogs. Can you see the pattern? Do you know where the thieves will strike next? Once you have verified your solution, draw a picture of the pooch that almost got pinched on the Missing Dog's Report (p. 16).

World Map

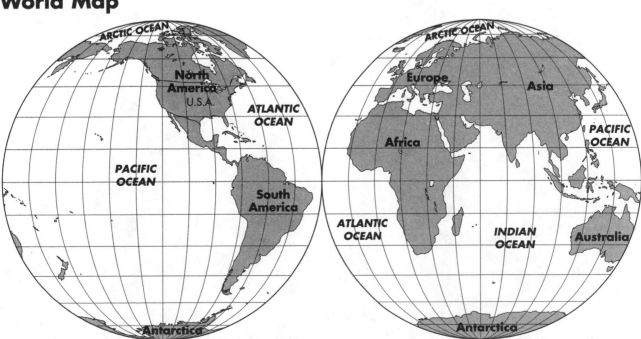

Missing Dog's Report

Tue, Rhodesian ridgeback
Dakar

Buttons, Welsh corgi
London

Nininha, poodle
Brasilia

Teddy, American cocker spaniel
Washington, D.C.

Chu Nyo, chow chow
Seoul

ABBREVIATED ARTIST

Or Identifying Map Abbreviations

The Mystery

"I am a desperate man!" Juan Palazzo shouted, tossing his hat and overcoat on an empty chair. "You must help me or I'll be ruined! Finished!"

Detectives Hyde and Seek hastily exchanged glances. "Of course we'll help you, if we can," Seek said, offering the man a glass of water. "Drink this, sit down, and tell us about your problem."

Señor Palazzo gratefully took the glass and sat down. "I am an art dealer. Last month I sold a brilliant work of art—Paletto's Birds of a Feather—to a Mr. and Mrs. Ochre. Now they are accusing me of selling them a forgery! I handle all of Paletto's work! Why would I sell them a forgery of one of my own artists?"

Detective Hyde raised an eyebrow. "There seems to be a simple solution to all of this. Have Paletto look at the painting and assure everyone that it's an original."

Señor Palazzo threw back his head and bitterly laughed. "That's what I thought too! Unfortunately, no one has seen Pablo Paletto in three weeks! I've checked everywhere—no Pablo. But in his studio I found this note." Palazzo handed a small white envelope to Detective Seek. "He wrote it in English! I thought I knew English pretty well but there are several words he uses that I've never seen before. I think it's a code of some kind. I was hoping you could figure it out and find Paletto before the Ochres have me arrested!"

Seek read the note aloud. "To Whom it May Concern: I need time alone to finish my latest masterpiece, Bird's Eye View. I prefer not to be disturbed except in case of an emergency. You'll find me at a cabin in Eagle Mt., N.C. There is no telephone so you'll have to come and contact me in person. Here are the directions from Eagle Mt., N.C., to the cabin: Head north on Hwy. 68. Turn right onto Songbird Pkwy.

Take your first left onto Cardinal St. You'll cross Sparrow R. Then turn right onto Oriole Rd. Go to the end of the road and turn left onto Hummingbird Ln. Take the first right onto Wren Cv. Follow signs to Blue Jay Pt. At Swan Lk., rent a boat and row out to Robin Isl. My cabin is right up from the dock."

Detective Seek smiled. "It's not in code," she said. "Paletto has used abbreviations. All we need is a map and we can pinpoint Paletto's exact location."

Can you?

Use the Clues

Often people use abbreviations, or shortened forms of words, to describe map terms. Look at Paletto's directions and the map. Can you figure out the abbreviations and trace your way to the artist? Then, read each abbreviation below and fill in the blank with the word it represents.

Directions to cabin in Eagle Mt., N.C.: Head north on Hwy. 68. Turn right onto Songbird Pkwy. Take first left onto Cardinal St. You'll cross Sparrow R. and then turn right onto Oriole Rd. Go to the end of the road and turn left onto Hummingbird Ln. Take the first right onto Wren Cv. Follow signs to Blue Jay Pt. At Swan Lk., rent a boat and row out to Robin Isl. My cabin is right up from the dock.

1. Mt. _____

2. N.C. _____

3. Hwy. _____

4. Pkwy. _____

5. St. _____

6. R. _____

7. Rd. _____

8. Ln. _____

9. Cv. _____

10. Pt. _____

11. Lk. _____

12. Isl. _____

Name_____

Eagle Mountain, North Carolina

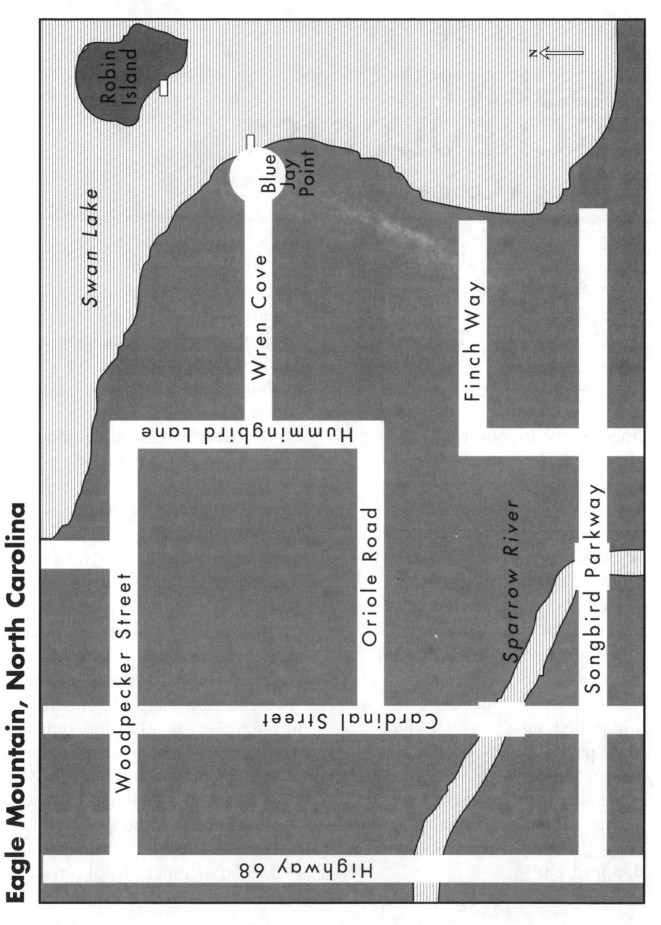

THE CASE OF THE

ABSENT ARCHEOLOGIST

Or Using a Compass Rose

The Mystery

Professor Carbon Dating nervously fingered the lock on his briefcase. "In here is the last recorded communication from Dr. Rosetta Stone," he said in a solemn voice. "As you know," he continued, "it has been over one month since Dr. Stone was last seen!"

Detective Hyde cleared his throat. "We understand your concern Professor Dating. Why don't you show us the note she left?"

Dating quickly unlocked the case and pulled out a piece of yellow lined paper. "As you can see," he began, "this paper has been used to make a pencil rubbing from an ancient tablet. Dr. Stone made this rubbing the day before she disappeared!"

Detective Hyde tapped the paper.

"Now let me get this straight. You and Dr. Stone were at an archeological dig in South America—the City in the Mist. A little over one month ago, Dr. Stone found this tablet and made a rubbing. Then what?"

"Well," confided Professor Dating, "Dr. Stone said the tablet gave directions to an ancient site— the famous City of the Sun! Legend has it that the City of the Sun was built with precious gems—rubies, diamonds, and sapphires! The next day, Stone and her backpack were gone!"

"Do you think she went in search of the city, Professor?" Seek asked.

"Most definitely!" the professor shouted. "And that's what worries me! You see, when I decoded the tablet, it gave directions in the form of a riddle. And I can't figure it out! How will I know if she's safe? What if she needs help?" he groaned.

"A riddle?" Hyde and Seek exclaimed together. "Say, Professor," said Hyde, "can you decode this

20

thing for us? Maybe we can figure it out."

"Certainly," said the professor. "I'll write it out for you."

In a few minutes he handed the paper to the detectives. Hyde and Seek studied the riddle. "Hmmm," murmured Seek. "Have you got a map showing where you were?" Professor Dating produced one and Hyde and Seek got busy.

"Oh Dear! What if she's wandering in the wilderness?" Professor Dating moaned.

"Calm down, Dating!" Hyde said impatiently. "If she used her map the right way she knew just where to go!"

"Where?" shouted Professor Dating excitedly.

Can you tell him?

THE RIDDLE . . .

Go south by southwest to the mouth of the snake.

Then west by northwest past the falls to a lake.

Next go north by northeast to the nose of a beast.

Then last (not least) travel east by southeast.

You'll see (if you can) that's where you began!

The path you have made is that which you seek.

Why not draw some lines and then take a peek?

In this city you'll find gems big and little.

Where is this city? Why it's right in the middle!

Professor Dating's Map

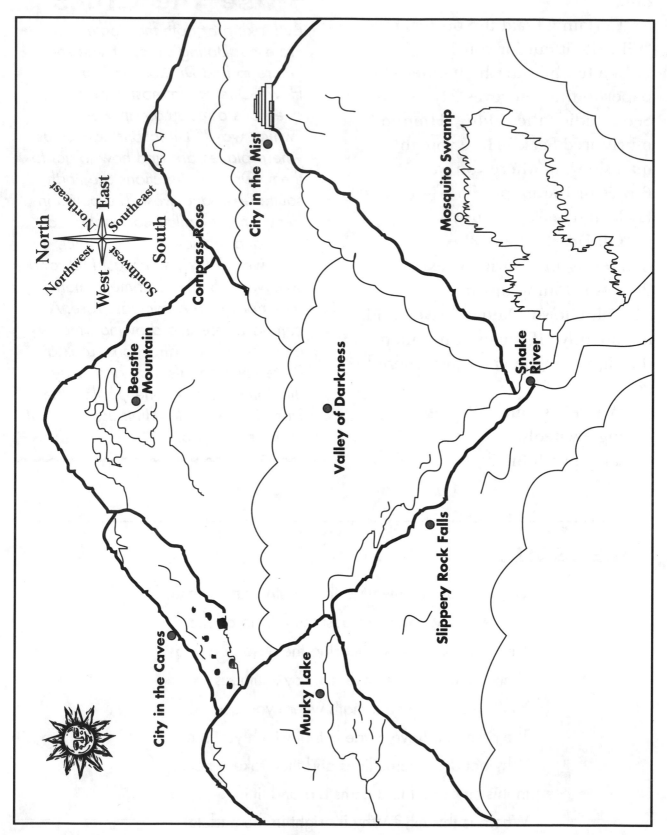

THE CASE OF THE

VANISHING SISTERS

Or Using a Grid Map

The Mystery

"I realize this is a little out of your line," began Captain Schwab of the Brown City Police Department, as he drove the unmarked police car down 32nd Street. "But here's the deal. The Museum of Art in Marconi, Italy, is missing the Five Sisters!"

Detective Hyde raised an eyebrow. "So, they made off with some sisters, eh? Anyone else in the family missing?" he asked.

Detective Seek hid a smile. "I believe the Five Sisters are five famous statues. Am I right, Captain?"

"Correct!" Schwab answered. "These statues were all carved by the famous sculptor Angelo Michelini hundreds of years ago. They're priceless! Our sources say that the Sisters were secretly shipped to Brown City last week. And they're somewhere in the neighborhood. The police department has only one lead, and we can't figure it out. That's why we need your help."

"What's the lead?" Hyde asked.

Schwab pulled out his notebook. "We got a tip this morning that the bingo hall on East 32nd Street would lead us in the right direction. The tip said to be there for the jackpot game at 8:00 P.M. So that's where we're heading."

A few minutes later they pulled into a crowded parking lot. Hyde, Seek, and Detective Schwab filed into a large hall. "Better buy some bingo cards to keep from drawing any attention to ourselves," Hyde whispered. "Let's get in line."

At the front of the line, a small, nervous man was seated at a desk selling bingo cards from a big stack. The line moved quickly and Hyde, Seek, and Schwab were soon seated at a table with their cards.

"I'm puzzled," Detective Seek whispered. "We were all given bingo cards from the pile. But the man in front of me was given a card from a small drawer in the desk."

"Hmmm...I smell a rat!" Captain Schwab growled. "Do you still see the guy?"

Seek pointed to a man sitting near the door. "He's the one!" she said. "Let's keep an eye on him!"

The game began. The man who sold the cards now turned a large plastic ball containing small chips. He stopped the ball and pulled out a chip. "N2," he called. Players marked their cards. The ball turned. "O7," he continued.

"Looks like our friend is pretty lucky," Hyde commented.

Indeed, the man by the door had yet to miss a call. The ball continued to turn. "I8...B3...G5."

"Bingo!" the man shouted. The other players groaned while he picked up his winning card and headed for the exit.

"Quick!" shouted Seek. "Stop that man. Once we get that bingo card and a map of the city we'll know where to find those missing statues!"

Do you?

Use the Clues

Detective Seek said that the bingo card and a map of the city would help locate the stolen statues. How can a map help you find the exact place you're looking for? Easily! Maps often are laid out in a grid pattern to help pinpoint a certain location. The grid lines that run north to south are given numbers, while the lines that run west to east are given letters. Locations are given a coordinate—such as D14. By running your finger along the D line and the 14 line, you can find the location by noting where the lines intersect. Look at the copy of the winning bingo card and the map of Brown City. Can you find the locations of the Five Sisters?

Name_____

Brown City

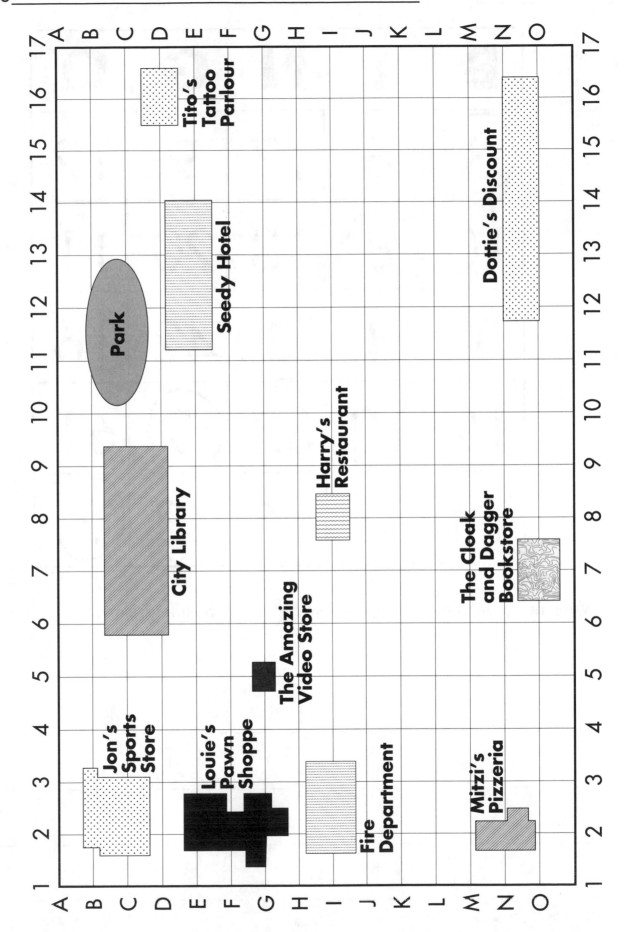

Name_____

B	I	N	G	O
③	6	17	9	12
10	⑧	13	20	11
1	4	②	42	16
19	18	37	⑤	61
14	31	15	43	⑦

Write the location of each of the Five Sisters on the lines below.

_____

_____

_____

_____

THE CASE OF THE
MISSING MILLIONAIRES
Or Determining Latitude and Longitude

The Mystery

"Are you sure we're off the boat?" Detective Hyde asked Detective Seek as she guided him unsteadily down the ramp of the S.S. Sardine. "I still feel like I'm going up and down...up and down..."

Detective Seek smiled. "Yes, we're off. I had no idea you got seasick!"

Suddenly Hyde stopped. "Hey! Isn't that Officer Blotter going up and down over there?" He pointed to several men gathered by two shiny black automobiles at the end of an empty boat pier.

"That's Officer Blotter all right!" answered Seek. "And he's not going up and down. It looks as if he's angry. Maybe we can help."

Officer Blotter greeted the two detectives with a shake of his head. "Where were you two when I needed you?" he sighed.

"We've been on a three-hour tour aboard the S.S. Sardine," Detective Seek explained. "What's happened?"

Officer Blotter made himself comfortable on the hood of one of the black cars. "Been tracing a husband and wife team of counterfeiters," he began. "William and Penelope Lottabuck—alias Bogus Bill and Bad Penny. Finally thought we had them caught at a fancy address in Currency Hills, where they've been posing as millionaires." Officer Blotter paused and nodded to a gentleman standing nearby. "When we paid the couple a visit this morning the butler, Mr. Greenbacks, said they had left town several days ago."

Greenbacks cleared his throat. "That's quite right, Officer. They claimed to be taking their boat out for a quick sail."

Detective Seek glanced at Detective Hyde. "Someone must have tipped them off," she said. "Is this the pier where they usually dock their boat?"

"Yes, madam," replied Greenbacks.

Detective Hyde raised an

eyebrow. "Any idea where they might have sailed?"

Greenbacks thought hard. "Well, the Lottabucks often spoke of an island hideaway. Rather private, you know?"

Officer Blotter looked grim. "The Pacific Ocean's mighty big," he said.

"Do these cars belong to the Lottabucks?" asked Detective Seek, pointing to the two shiny automobiles.

Greenbacks patted the bumper of one car fondly. "Yes, his and her Cadillacs," he answered. "Notice the license plates—HIS178E and HERS 18S! Because the cars are identical, it was the only way they could tell them apart. Rather handy!"

Detective Seek smiled. "I'll say it's handy!" she said, turning to Officer Blotter. "And if you've got a world atlas, those license plates will show us where the Lottabucks are headed!"

Do you know how?

Use the Clues

Fortunately, Officer Blotter had a world atlas in the glove compartment of his car. By using the map and the license plates, Detective Seek was able to pinpoint the Lottabucks' destination. How? First, she knew that every place on earth has a fixed location—a global address. Maps and globes have imaginary lines that form a grid pattern. Lines of latitude run north and south of the equator, while lines of longitude run east and west of the prime meridian. Each line is labeled with a degree symbol (°) and a direction. From the license plates on the Lottabucks' cars, Detective Seek guessed that 18S stood for a latitude reading of 18° (18 degrees) south and that 178E stood for a longitude reading of 178° (178 degrees) east. Using these coordinates, she was able to find out where the Lottabucks were headed. Can you? Use the license plates and the map to find the counterfeiters!

Latitude and Longitude Map

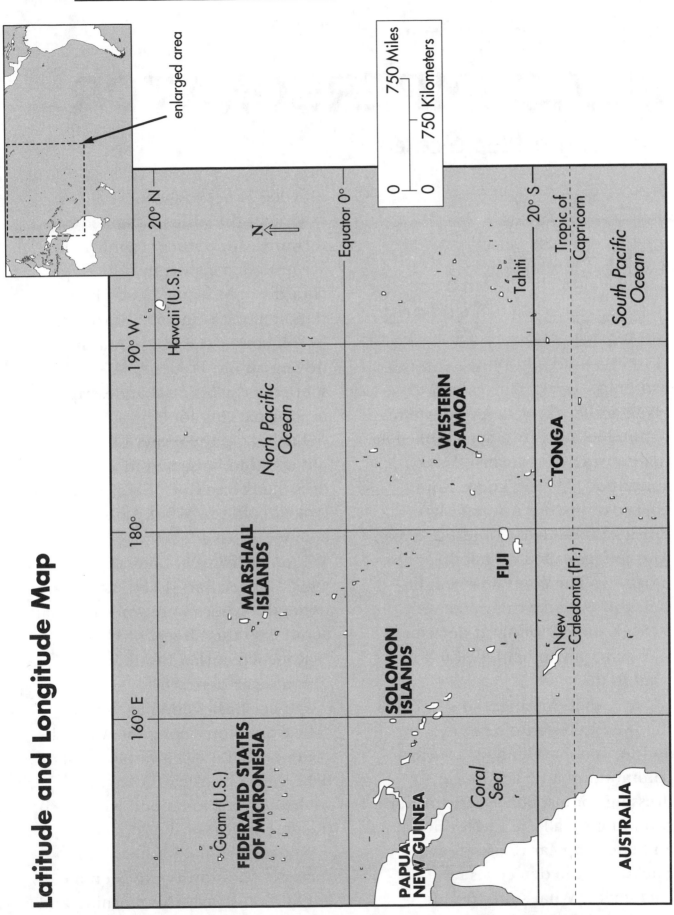

enlarged area

750 Miles
750 Kilometers

20° N

N

Equator 0°

20° S

190° W

180°

160° E

Hawaii (U.S.)

North Pacific
Ocean

MARSHALL
ISLANDS

FEDERATED STATES
OF MICRONESIA

Guam (U.S.)

SOLOMON
ISLANDS

PAPUA
NEW GUINEA

Coral
Sea

AUSTRALIA

New
Caledonia (Fr.)

FIJI

WESTERN
SAMOA

TONGA

Tahiti

Tropic of
Capricorn

South Pacific
Ocean

THE CASE OF THE
ELVIS IMPERSONATOR
Or Using a Map Scale

The Mystery

"I'm in a bind and I hope you two can help," Lucky Barnes said to Hyde and Seek, as he put down his lemonade. Detective Seek looked at her cousin with concern. Lucky continued. "As you know, I'm in charge of the 8th Annual Elvis Presley Look-Alike Contest this year. Two judges called in sick this morning. The contest is tonight. Can you two take their places?"

Seek smiled fondly at her cousin. "We're happy to help. Just tell us what to do."

Later that evening, the detectives followed Lucky into a large auditorium. Suddenly there was a commotion backstage in the dressing rooms. Police officers were rounding up all the Elvis contestants and checking car registrations. Lucky and the detectives ran backstage. "What's the trouble, officers?" Lucky asked.

One of the officers stepped forward. "I'm Officer Candy Barr. We just got a report in from Cape Girardeau, Missouri. A gasoline station along route 55 was robbed by someone dressed as Elvis and driving an old Pontiac! We've spotted a car fitting that description in your parking lot."

Backstage, the owner of the car was asked to be seated in a small dressing room. Ron "Elvis" Roncoco looked baffled. "What's this all about?" he asked.

"You're from St. Louis, aren't you?" Officer Barr asked. Roncoco nodded. "Where were you earlier, at about 2:00 this afternoon?"

Roncoco curled his upper lip. "On my way here. So?"

Officer Barr folded her arms. "Make any stops along the way?" she continued. "Like at a gasoline station near Cape Girardeau? One was robbed earlier today and you match the description of the robber."

Roncoco shook his head with surprise. "Couldn't have been me. I left St. Louis early this morning and drove straight through. Filled up my gasoline tank before I left!"

Detective Seek smiled and glanced out of the window that faced the parking lot. "You've got a real classic automobile, Mr. Roncoco. Is it a '57 Pontiac or a '58?"

Roncoco beamed proudly. "1957! A genuine 1957 Pontiac. She's old but still gets about 10 miles to the gallon."

Seek looked surprised. "Really! With what, a 30-gallon fuel tank?"

Roncoco scoffed. "Heck no! it's only a 20-gallon one." Suddenly his eyes narrowed. "Say, what are you getting at?" he asked.

Without answering, Detective Seek took a travel-sized atlas from her purse. Using a ruler, she made some calculations on a scrap of paper. Tapping her pencil on the map she looked at Officer Barr. "I believe you've found your man," Seek remarked. "Mr. Roncoco is lying. There's no way he could have driven from St. Louis to Memphis without running out of gas."

How does she know?

Use the Clues

Detective Seek used a ruler and a travel atlas to prove that Ron Roncoco was lying. How? A travel atlas contains road maps of different places to help people find the best way to get where they are going. Every map includes a map scale that helps travelers determine how far one place is from another.

By using a strip of paper with a straight edge, you can figure out the distances between any two places. Here's how: First, find the map scale. This will tell you how many inches on a map represent the actual number of miles or kilometers on the earth. Use the piece of paper to trace the scale. (You may want to mark the halfway point as well as the beginning and the end.) Then, lay the piece of paper along the road you wish to measure. Mark and count the number of inches between the two cities. Multiply that number by the number of miles on the scale. This will give you an approximation of the actual distance between the two cities.

Next, you'll need to determine the vehicle range, the distance a car can travel before running out of gas. To do this, find out the vehicle's tank size. Next, determine how many miles the car can travel per gallon. Multiply the two numbers to find out how far the car can go without running out of gas.

Detective Seek heard Roncoco say that he filled his car with gas in St. Louis before he left for Memphis. Because she knew that his car could only hold 20 gallons of gasoline and could travel 10 miles per gallon, Seek figured that Roncoco had to be lying. How? Use the road map of Missouri and Tennessee to find out. (Hint: First compute the distance between the two cities, then find the vehicle range of Roncoco's car.)

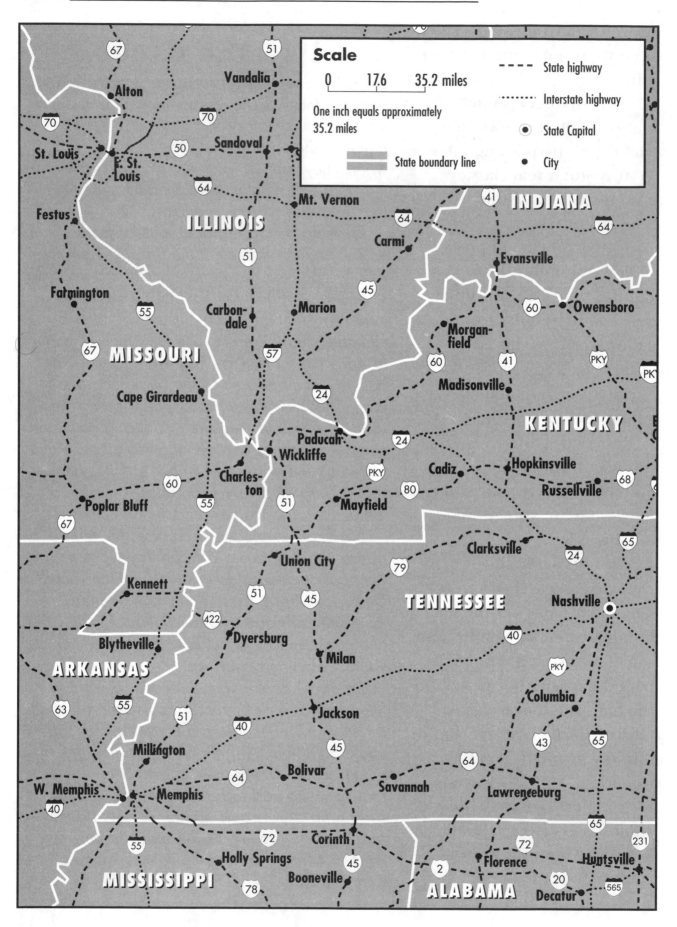

THE CASE OF THE
SMILING SEÑORITA
Or Comparing Time Zones

The Mystery

"So, how do you like our city?" Captain Phineas Schwab of the New York City Police Department asked Detectives Hyde and Seek as they settled down in his office.

"Police departments seem the same wherever you go," laughed Detective Hyde, removing his hat. "Your twin brother Elias sends his greetings. It was very nice of him to suggest we pay you a visit on our trip to New York for the Private Detective Convention."

Captain Schwab smiled. "Good old Elias," he beamed.

Suddenly the captain's intercom buzzed. "Michael Fey's here. Should I bring him in?" a voice asked.

Captain Schwab frowned. "Give me a minute," he said. Hyde and Seek got up.

"We see you're busy," Seek said. "We can come back later."

Captain Schwab gave her a wink. "Go ahead and sit down. This case is a real mystery. This guy, Michael Fey—alias Michael the Fox—is here for questioning in connection with an art theft in England two weeks ago. A valuable painting called the Smiling Señorita was stolen from the Duke of Worcestershire's house during the noon-time royal wedding. London Police think Fey did it.

"Why?" questioned Detective Seek.

Captain Schwab explained. "Fey, at one time, was Europe's most infamous cat burglar. Ten years ago he was caught and spent four years in prison. Since then, he has moved to New York and started his own travel agency. Very successful too. We've got nothing to pin on him but London says he left his trademark—a red rose—at the scene of the crime." Captain Schwab frowned. "Only problem is, he says he was here in New York City at the time. I've questioned him over and over and his testimony never changes. Listen to what he says.

Maybe you two can figure something out."

Detectives Hyde and Seek sat back down as a tall, thin man was led into the room. Captain Schwab offered him a chair. "Okay Michael, let's try it again," he began. "Where were you on the day in question?"

Fey smiled at the group in the office. "On the day in question I was in my apartment in New York City. I woke up at 6:00 A.M. and had an early morning jog in Central Park. I returned to my apartment at about 6:45. No one saw me leave or return to the building." Michael paused and looked over at Hyde and Seek. "You see, I prefer to use the fire escape. Old habits are hard to break, I guess! Anyway, when I returned I worked on my book, *My Life in Crime*, for several hours. At 12:00 noon I fixed myself a light lunch and settled down in front of the T.V. to watch the broadcast of the royal wedding—live from London. I saw the entire wedding and, after supper, went to bed at about 9:00 P.M."

Captain Schwab shook his head. "All right, Michael, please wait outside while I discuss a few things with my colleagues." When Michael Fey closed the door Captain Schwab glanced at Hyde and Seek. "See? Always the same testimony. It can't be proved or disproved."

"Oh, I don't know about that," Detective Seek said. "The Fox is lying and any time zone map can prove it!"

How?

Use the Clues

Detective Seek said that a time zone map could prove that Michael the Fox had lied in his testimony. What is a time zone map? What does it show? Because of the earth's rotation, the sun shines on different places on the globe at different times. Since it takes one day, or 24 hours, for the earth to make a complete turn, or rotation, the world has been divided into 24 time zones— one for each hour of the day. Each time zone is laid out along every 15 degrees of longitude, starting at the prime meridian at Greenwich, England. Now to solve the mystery, look at Michael Fey's testimony and the time zone map. Can you prove that Fey is lying?

Name_____

Testimony of Michael the Fox

On the day in question I was in my apartment in New York City. I woke up at 6:00 A.M. and had an early morning jog in Central Park. I returned to my apartment at about 6:45. No one saw me leave or return to the building. You see, I prefer to use the fire escape. Old habits are hard to break, I guess! Anyway, when I returned I worked on my book, My Life in Crime, for several hours. At 12:00 noon I fixed myself a light lunch and settled down in front of the T.V. to watch the broadcast of the royal wedding—live from London. I saw the entire wedding and, after supper, went to bed at about 9:00 P.M.

International Date Line
midnight
12 11 10 9 8 7 6 5 4 3 2 1 Noon 11 10 9 8 7 6 5 4 3 2 1 12

180° 165° 150° 135° 120° 105° 90° 75° 60° 45° 30° 15° 0° 15° 30° 45° 60° 75° 90° 105° 120° 135° 150° 165° 180°

International Date Line
midnight

Prime Meridian

EAST

WEST

• Peking
Fiji •
• Sydney

• Moscow
• Vienna
• Cairo

London •

Direction of earth's rotation

New York City •
Washington, D.C. •
Juneau •
Honolulu •
Samoa •

MISSING MONSTER

Or Reading a Contour Map

The Mystery

"Now see here, Detective Hyde," Lady Edwina Rake began impatiently. "I'm prepared to pay you and your partner all sorts of money. But I need you to find that creature as quickly as possible!"

Detective Hyde rubbed his eyes wearily. "Yes, Lady Rake. So you've told us. However, finding a missing abominable snowman isn't really our line of business."

Lady Edwina sniffed. "Let me explain it again. My husband, Lord Hugo Rake, is a world famous mountain climber. During his last trip up Mount Monstrosity, he had a frightening encounter with an abominable snowman. However, no one believes him. His career is in ruins! You've got to find that creature and prove to the world that Hugo is not a liar. I've got my husband's papers with me," she said, shuffling through a leather brief case. Pulling a sheet out, she smiled triumphantly at the detectives. "Here is his description of what happened. Read it yourself!"

Detective Seek read the paper aloud: "On the morning of August 19th, I, Lord Rake, awoke from a sound sleep when someone or something disturbed my climbing gear. It was shortly before sunrise. As I quietly looked out of my tent, I saw the dim outline of a massive creature going through my equipment bags. I took my rifle and crept up behind the beast. As the sun continued to rise, I could make out a horrible hairy figure. It was about 7 feet tall, ape-like in appearance, and covered with coarse orange hair. When it saw me, it dropped my bag and took off down a sloping hill. I shall never forget the sight of the creature running straight toward the rising sun! It continued down the side of the mountain for some time, with me in hot pursuit. I finally lost the beast in the thick woods. Signed, Lord Hugo Rake."

Detective Seek closed her eyes for several seconds. "Lady Rake," she asked, "do you happen to have a map of the mountain that Hugo was on at the time?"

Lady Edwina began digging in the brief case again. "Certainly," she said, handing the detectives a neatly folded contour map. "Will this help? My husband's camp site is marked by the X."

Hyde and Seek spread the map out on the desk. "Yes it does," Hyde answered. "But I'm afraid you don't need us after all. According to this map, your husband isn't telling the truth!"

How does he know?

Use the Clues

Lady Edwina provided the detectives with Lord Hugo's testimony as well as with a contour map of Mount Monstrosity. Contour maps show landforms and use lines or color to show different elevations. Elevation is the height of land above sea level.

A contour line on a map connects areas that have the same elevation. Most contour lines are drawn in irregular circles. Contour intervals are the spaces between the circles. They show variation in elevation. Widely spaced contour lines mean that the land is flat or gently sloping. A steep slope, or mountainside, is shown by lines drawn close together. Now look at both Lord Hugo's testimony and the map of Mount Monstrosity. How does Detective Hyde know that Lord Hugo is lying? (Hint: use the compass rose and think of where the sun rises and sets!)

Lord Hugo Rake's Sworn Testimony:

On the morning of August 19th, I, Lord Rake awoke from a sound sleep when someone or something disturbed my climbing gear. It was shortly before sunrise. As I quietly looked out of my tent, I saw the dim outline of a massive creature going through my equipment bags. I took my rifle and crept up behind the beast. As the sun continued to rise, I could make out a horrible hairy figure. It was about 7 feet tall, ape-like in appearance, and covered with coarse orange hair. When it saw me, it dropped my bag and took off down the sloping hill. I shall never forget the sight of the creature running straight toward the rising sun! It continued down the side of the mountain for some time, with me in hot pursuit. I finally lost the beast in the thick woods.

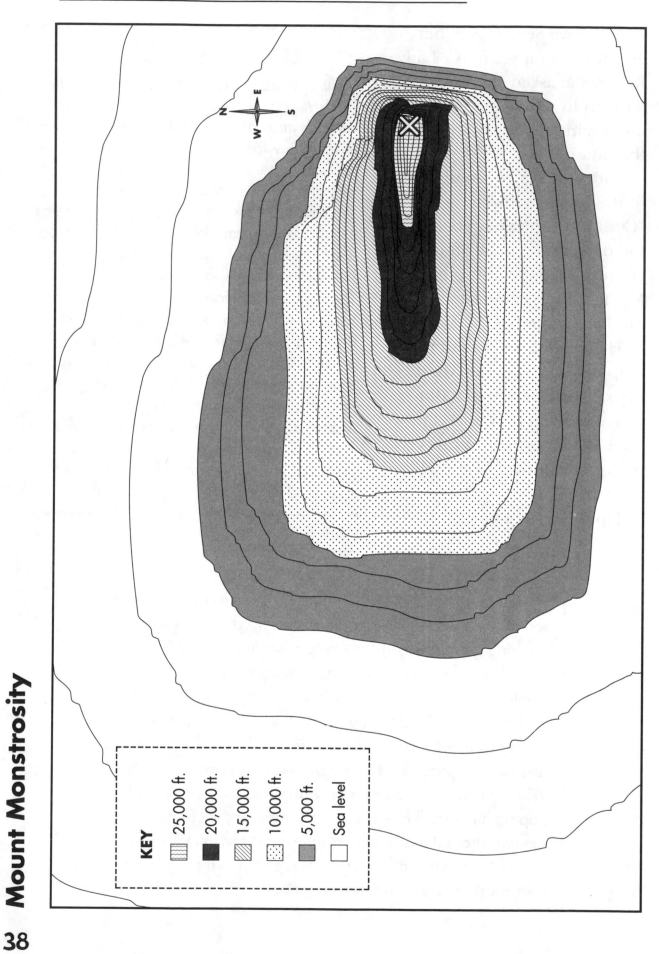

Mount Monstrosity

KEY

- ▨ 25,000 ft.
- ■ 20,000 ft.
- ▨ 15,000 ft.
- ▨ 10,000 ft.
- ▨ 5,000 ft.
- ☐ Sea level

THE CASE OF THE
RANSOMED ROCKER
Or Using a Street Map

The Mystery

"Have you seen all the headlines?" Detective Seek asked Detective Hyde, as they drove to the Brown City Police Department. "Pic's disappearance is big news!"

"Pic?" Detective Hyde looked puzzled. "Who's that?" he asked.

"I can't believe you've never heard of Pic and the Amplifiers," Seek said in a surprised tone. "Why, they're one of the biggest rock 'n' roll groups around. Pic is considered the world's best left-handed bass player. He's been missing since Saturday."

"Who'd name a kid Pic?" Detective Hyde muttered.

Later, at the police station, Captain Schwab got down to business. "Listen," he began. "Every teenager in the state is on my back for not finding this Pic guy. We've investigated every lead and have gotten nowhere. I need your help." Schwab turned to a young woman dressed completely in black. "This is Pinky Ring. She's the last person who saw Pic before he disappeared."

Pinky Ring looked at the detectives, her eyes overflowing with tears. "I'm in mourning!" she cried. "Something bad has happened to Pic! I just feel it...here!" She pressed a hand against her heart.

"Why don't you tell us what you know," Detective Hyde suggested.

Pinky closed her eyes tightly. "I can see it all as if it were yesterday," she whispered. "You see, I'm Pic's absolute biggest fan! I practically live outside his town house! I know his every move! On Saturday I waited outside Pic's place until he came out at about 10:00 A.M. I followed him as he turned east onto Laser Light Lane, and then south onto 4th Street where he went into CD's Record World. He came out with Buzz Bomber's latest CD at about 10:30. He then headed west on Hot Licks Boulevard and south on 3rd Street to Tune's Guitars. Through the window, I saw him trying out some new left-handed bass guitars. At about 11:00 he left the store and someone asked him for an autograph. He took off his left glove and signed his name. Then he gave the girl his nail-studded glove! I just died with envy!" Pinky paused, her eyes shining at the memory. "Well, then he walked down to the corner of 3rd Street and Heavy Metal Avenue. He turned east on Heavy Metal and walked to Metallica's Fashion World where he bought a pair of gold pants. At 11:30 he continued east on Heavy Metal Avenue and went into the Twisted Scissors Hair Salon for his weekly trim. At 12:00 noon he came down the steps and was asked for his autograph again. When he took off his other glove to sign his name, I asked if I could have it. He then turned north on 6th Street and headed to Java Joe's Café. That's when something happened! He went into the café but never came out!"

Hyde glanced at Seek. "Are you sure Pinky?" he asked. "Maybe he went out a back door."

Pinky sobbed "Java Joe's doesn't have a back door. Or windows either! The only person who came out was a woman with a large shopping bag. After a couple of hours I went in to look for him and he wasn't there! That's when I called his agent and the police."

Captain Schwab shrugged. "We've been all over Java Joe's—clean as a whistle."

Seek looked puzzled. "Pinky, do you have the glove Pic gave you?" she asked.

"Of course!" Pinky cried, pulling the nail-studded black leather glove from her pocket.

"Pinky! You said he took this glove off to sign an autograph, right?" Seek questioned.

"Yeah, so?" Pinky sniffed.

Seek slapped the glove against Captain Schwab's desk. "This is a right-handed glove! The Pic who gave you this was an impostor! Let's look at the map of the city. Forget Java Joe's. I'll show you where Pic was really last seen!" Can you?

Use the Clues

A city map can be a very helpful tool in locating a specific place or address. How about a missing rock musician? Remember that Pic was a famous left-handed guitar player. Chances are that if he played guitar with his left hand he wrote with his left hand as well. Since Detective Seek knew that the real Pic would never sign his name with his right hand she figured that somewhere along the route the real Pic vanished and an impostor appeared. Look at the map of Pic's neighborhood. Then, use the compass rose and follow Pinky's directions to pinpoint Pic's last-known whereabouts.

The Case of the Ransomed Rocker

NOTES:

1. Pic leaves town house. Heads east on Laser Light Lane.

2. He turns south on 4th Street and enters CD's Record World.

3. From CD's Record World, Pic heads west on Hot Licks Boulevard.

4. He then turns south on 3rd Street to Tune's Guitars.

5. Outside of Tune's, Pic signs an autograph.

6. Then Pic continues south on 3rd to Heavy Metal Avenue. He heads east to Metallica's Fashion World.

7. He continues east to the Twisted Scissors Hair Salon.

8. Pic leaves the hair salon, signs another autograph, and turns north on 6th Street.

9. He enters Java Joe's Café. According to Pinky Ring, he does not leave.

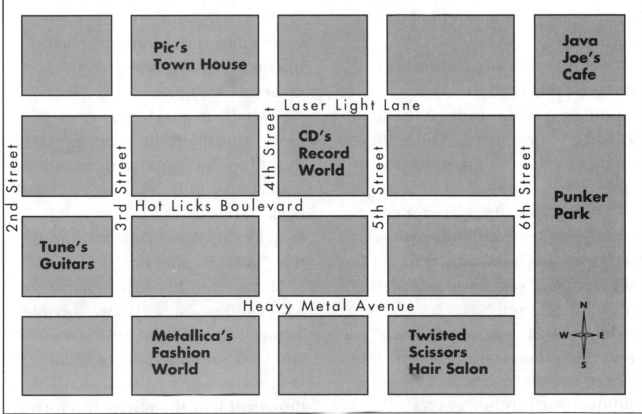

THE CASE OF THE
MISSING MICROCHIP
Or Reading a Road Map

The Mystery

"This is a matter of the utmost importance," Dexter Seek whispered to his sister. "I know I can trust you and your partner to keep quiet."

Detective Seek shook her head. "For heaven's sake, Dex," she began, "cut the melodrama and tell us how we can help."

"Well," he began cautiously, "my contact is missing!"

Detective Hyde scanned the floor of Dexter's apartment. "Gosh, they can be murder to find, especially in a shag rug!"

"Not a contact lens," snapped Dexter. "My contact—someone who has important information to tell me! Her code name is 'Hata Mari' and she's missing!"

Detective Hyde's mouth hung open. "You mean you're a spy?" He glanced at Detective Seek. "You never told me your brother was a spy!"

Dexter continued: "Hata arrived here by airplane several nights ago and was staying in a hotel in Flight City. When I got to her room yesterday morning she was gone. The place had been ransacked. All I could find were these." Dexter produced a pair of shattered eye glasses. "I am desperate to get her back. Can you help?"

Suddenly they all heard a quiet knock on the door. Dexter leapt to his feet. "Who is it?" he demanded.

"Ducks fly south for the winter!" a voice answered. Dexter hurriedly opened the door and pulled in a disheveled woman.

"Hata!" he gasped. An odor of moth balls filled the room as Hata moved to the couch and looked suspiciously at Detectives Hyde and Seek.

"They're okay," Dexter assured her. "What happened?"

Hata rested her head against the back of the couch. "It was horrible. Thugs from XTREM grabbed me and took me to a hideout. They kept me in a closet! You see, they thought I had the microchip with me and I did! But I hid it under a floorboard in the closet before they searched me."

"How did you escape?" Hyde asked.

"The smell of moth balls from the closet got to be too much for me. And I started to cough uncontrollably. They took me outside to get some air and I managed to slip away into the woods. I stumbled around for hours until I found a small cabin. From there I called a taxi and here I am. By the way, can you pay the taxi? It's waiting outside."

Dexter quickly paid the taxi driver and opened several windows. "That smell is pretty bad," he admitted. "And I suppose the microchip is still in the closet. Can you lead us to it?"

Hata shook her head. "I'm afraid it may be difficult. You see, I broke my glasses in the struggle in the hotel room so I couldn't read the road signs. But I was wearing my combination wristwatch and compass. And I can tell you what sounds I heard, like traffic and construction noises. I did see other cars—that could tell us whether I was on a major highway or a single-lane road."

Detective Seek took out a pen and wrote down all that Hata could remember. Dexter glanced at the list. "This may not be enough to go on," he remarked.

"Nonsense!" Detective Hyde said. "Get out a road map and we can pinpoint that hideout in a hurry!"

Can you?

Use the Clues

Detective Hyde said he could pinpoint the location of the hideout by using a road map and Hata's description. A road map is very useful for people who are traveling by car, truck, bus, or even bicycle. The legend, or key, explains what the symbols used on the map mean. The map scale shows how far it is from one place to another. By following Hata's description and using a highway map, Detective Hyde traced the route the thieves took to the hideout. Look at Hata's description. Then use the map key and scale to trace the way to XTREM's secret hiding place.

Name _____

The Case of the Missing Microchip

Left Flight City and headed south for about 10 miles; turned and headed east for about 10 miles. Turned left and headed north on major highway; crossed bridge and road construction. Made right turn heading east on double-lane road. After about 20 miles boarded a ferry. Crossed river and drove east for about 4 miles. Then turned south and drove for about 10 miles down a single-lane road. Turned left and drove down an unpaved dirt road. Went into house.

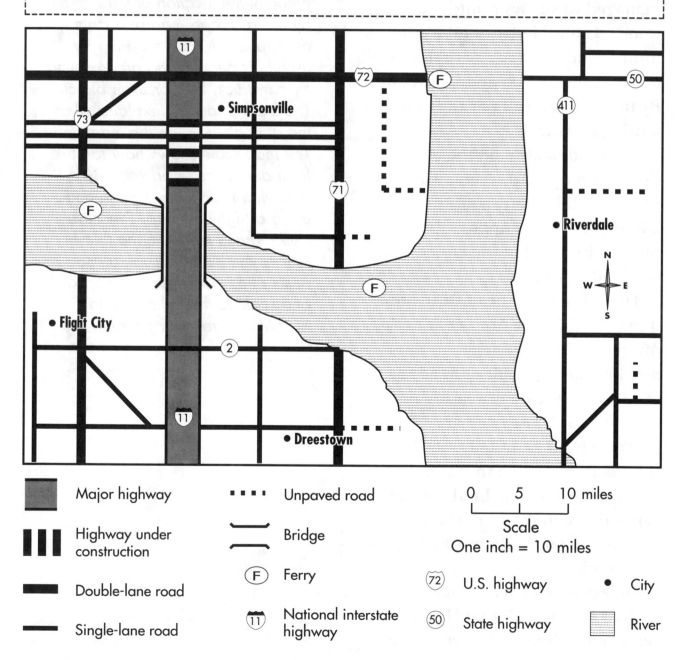

	Major highway	····	Unpaved road				
‖‖‖	Highway under construction	⏝	Bridge				
▬	Double-lane road	Ⓕ	Ferry	72	U.S. highway	•	City
—	Single-lane road	11	National interstate highway	50	State highway		River

Scale
0   5   10 miles
One inch = 10 miles

THE CASE OF THE
SNATCHED SCIENTIST
Or Reading a Resource Map

The Mystery

Elias Goldbug, federal investigator, stared intently at the two detectives seated before him. "It's extremely important that we get Professor Fermenti back," he said gravely. "The future of the world depends on it!" Detective Hyde removed his hat and glanced at Detective Seek. The investigator continued. "Professor Carla Fermenti has just completed a formula that could end world hunger forever!"

"Wonderful!" exclaimed Detective Hyde. "But how?"

Investigator Goldbug smiled. "The formula turns any type of dirt or sand into fertile soil. Anything can grow in it. Early this morning, Professor Carlo Fermenti was kidnapped! They broke the lock to his apartment with this." Goldbug picked up a small knife and handed it to Detective Seek.

"Looks like an oyster knife," she said.

Investigator Goldbug nodded. "Apparently, the kidnappers want to use the formula for profit. Sell it to the highest bidder!"

"That's terrible!" Detective Hyde muttered. "But I'm confused. Is the professor's name Carla or Carlo?"

Investigator Goldbug nervously adjusted his tie. "Both," he stated. "Unfortunately the kidnappers made off with the wrong Professor Fermenti. They snatched Carlo Fermenti—Carla's father. But Carla's the scientist who created the formula. Once the kidnappers realized their mistake, they sent Carla this ransom note." Goldbug handed a scrap of wrinkled brown paper to the detectives.

Hyde read the note aloud: "Dear professor Fermenti: We have your father. If you want to see him again, hand over the formula. You'll be hearing from us."

"Something smells fishy to me," Hyde commented.

Investigator Goldbug sighed. "The whole thing's fishy, if you ask me!"

Hyde shook his head and sniffed the ransom note. "I mean the note smells fishy. Looks like the kind of paper you wrap fish in."

Investigator Goldbug took the paper back. "Anyway, the kidnappers called Carla Fermenti at her house a couple of hours ago, but she wasn't at home. We got this message off her answering machine."

The investigator inserted a small cassette into a tape player and pushed "play." A low voice could be heard: "Listen, Fermenti, your old man's going to play ball with us. He says he knows most of the formula. Help him out and maybe you'll see him again."

And then, another voice: "Carla, honey, listen, it's Dad. I've figured out the barium, potassium, erbium, and cobalt. What's the rest? We'll call again later. I . . ." The professor's last words were lost in the sound of a loud factory whistle blowing in the background. The message ended.

"Now here's the mystery," the investigator began, tapping his pencil on the tape player. "Carla says the elements her father listed have nothing to do with the formula—or anything else for that matter. We're stumped. That's why we called you."

Detective Seek furrowed her brow. "Barium, potassium, erbium,

and cobalt...the chemical symbols for those elements are Ba, K, Er, and Co. Do you suppose the professor was trying to tell his daughter where he was?"

"Of course!" shouted Hyde. "Baker County! That's north of here. And with the other clues the kidnappers gave us, we should be able to find Professor Fermenti!"

Investigator Goldbug looked confused. "What other clues?" he asked.

Detective Seek smiled. "The oyster knife, the ransom note, and the factory whistle. All we need now is a resource map of Baker County and this mystery is solved!"

Do you know how?

Name_____

Use the Clues

Detective Seek said that the oyster knife, the ransom note, the factory whistle, and a resource map of Baker County would solve the mystery. How? A resource map uses symbols to show the most important products made or grown in an area. The map legend, or key, explains what each symbol represents. Look at the resource map of Baker County. Now remember each of the clues: an oyster knife, a fishy smelling ransom note, and the sound of a factory whistle. Where do you think Professor Fermenti is being held?

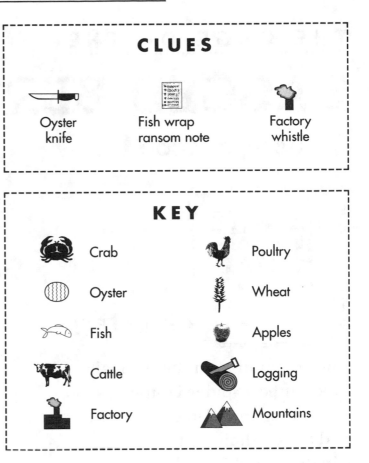

CLUES

Oyster knife

Fish wrap ransom note

Factory whistle

KEY

Crab

Oyster

Fish

Cattle

Factory

Poultry

Wheat

Apples

Logging

Mountains

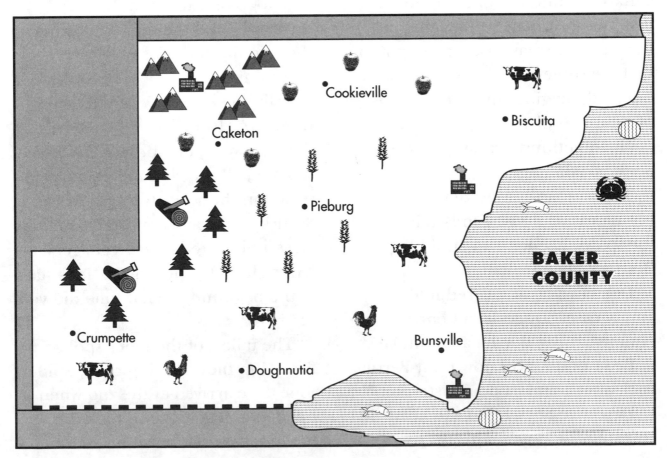

THE CASE OF THE
BAGGED BERTHA
Or Using a Zoo Map

The Mystery

The commotion in the normally quiet Insect/Spider House was too much to ignore. Detectives Hyde and Seek, admiring the zoo's stinkbug exhibit, looked up to see a distraught woman rummaging through a display case. "She's got to be here somewhere!" the woman moaned, digging through mounds of sand and dirt.

"Is something wrong?" Detective Seek asked.

The woman buried her head in her hands. "I'll say! I'm Bea Hive—the spider keeper. I'm afraid Big Bertha's been stolen!"

Detective Hyde peered into the empty case. "Dugesiella hentzi. Hmmm, is Big Bertha a tarantula?"

Bea nodded. "I know I put Bertha back after that last demonstration."

Detective Seek lifted the heavy lid covering the cage. "This isn't

locked. Could Bertha have crawled out?" she asked.

Bea shook her head. "I'm afraid not. I was giving a special demonstration to members of the Spider Club and I broke the latch of the display case by accident. Only the Spider Club would know that. I'll bet one of the club members took Bertha! They are all wearing matching yellow tee shirts with the club logo on them. I'm having security round them up and bring them to the zoo office for questioning!"

"Mind if we sit in?" asked Detective Hyde. "We're detectives. Perhaps we can help."

Later, all the club members were seated in the security guard's office. Security Officer Mumford crossed his arms and looked at the teenagers. "All right kids," he began, "let's start at the beginning. What time did you get here?"

The tallest of the teens spoke up first. "I'm the club president, Spider Jones. We arrived at the zoo when it opened at 9:00 A.M. We took our lunches and drinks to the picnic area and then went straight to the Insect/Spider House. Ms. Hive gave the demonstration, which ended at about 10:00. I took Harry to the first aid station because he felt dizzy. The other guys went their own separate ways. We were supposed to meet back at the picnic area at 11:00. Hugo was the first one there, and the rest of us came at about 11:15—except for Milton. He was late."

Milton looked nervous. "Hey!" he sputtered. "It took longer to feed the lions than I thought it would."

One by one, Officer Mumford asked each member to tell his story. Chuck and Bart said they walked straight to the Aviary for the birds of paradise show, claiming they missed the first few minutes. Milton and Hugo boarded the zoo tram at stop #2. Milton said he got off at stop #4 and watched the lion feeding at the Big Cats' House. Hugo said he rode the tram to stop #5 where he watched the monkey show. No one admitted to having taken the tarantula.

Security Officer Mumford rubbed his chin thoughtfully. "I guess we'll just have to search you boys," he said.

Detective Hyde cleared his throat. "That won't be necessary, Officer," he said, tossing a zoo brochure in front of Mumford. According to this, one of the boys is lying!"

Who is it?

Use the Clues

Zoos often provide visitors with a map showing the location of each exhibit. Detective Hyde said that the map could prove that one of the boys was lying. How? Reread the boys' stories. Then, using the zoo map, key, and schedule of the day's events, find out who's not telling the truth. (Hint: remember that the zoo tram leaves stop #1 on the hour and makes stops every ten minutes!)

THE MYSTERY OF THE BAGGED BERTHA

The tram leaves stop #1 on the hour and makes stops every ten minutes.

Today's Zoo Schedule

Polar ice show:
9:00–9:30

Birds of paradise show:
10:00–10:30

Monkey show:
10:00–10:30

Big cats' feeding time:
10:35–10:55

Reptile demonstration:
12:00–12:30

Elephant show:
2:00–2:30

Enjoy!

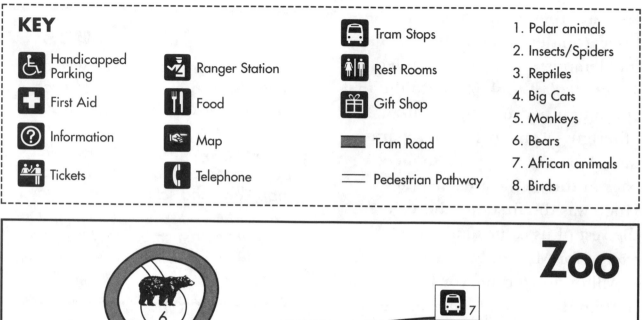

KEY

Handicapped Parking

First Aid

Information

Tickets

Ranger Station

Food

Map

Telephone

Tram Stops

Rest Rooms

Gift Shop

Tram Road

Pedestrian Pathway

1. Polar animals
2. Insects/Spiders
3. Reptiles
4. Big Cats
5. Monkeys
6. Bears
7. African animals
8. Birds

Zoo

Picnic Area

Parking Lot

Parking Lot

Parking Lot

THE CASE OF THE

MISSING MUMMY

Or Interpreting a Museum Map

The Mystery

Detective Hyde was fascinated with ancient Egypt. "Just wait until you see the Museum of History's new Egyptian exhibit!" he said to Detective Seek, as they made their way up the museum steps. "They have a scale model of the Great Pyramid that's over 30 feet tall! The actual pyramid in Egypt is considered the largest stone building ever constructed."

Detective Seek smiled. "Sounds exciting. Are you sure that Dr. Rogliphic won't mind taking us on a tour?" she asked. Dr. Hy Rogliphic was the museum curator and a close friend of Detective Hyde's.

"Not at all," Hyde replied as they entered the museum. "His office is over here."

From behind a closed door came the sound of shouting. Hyde timidly knocked on the door.

"Come in!" a voice demanded. Inside the room Dr. Rogliphic was seated behind his desk, with his head in hands. Next to the desk, a woman and a man stood glaring at each other.

"Hmmm, perhaps we should come back later," Seek said quietly.

Dr. Rogliphic looked up. "Detectives! Just what we need! Perhaps you two can help us solve this mystery," he said.

"What mystery?" Hyde asked, eyeing the two angry people.

Dr. Rogliphic stood up. "Let me introduce you. Detectives Hyde and Seek, this is our security guard Tom Manx, and my assistant, Ming Vaz. It seems that sometime last night one of our Egyptian mummies disappeared. Mr. Manx feels that Ms. Vaz took it."

"I did not!" Ms. Vaz shouted, pounding the desk. "Manx took it! I'm sure of it. He's been hanging around that mummy ever since the exhibit opened. He collects cat things—statues, books, portraits, everything. He told me himself! The mummy was of a cat. One of the pharaoh's own, we think!"

Mr. Manx grew red in the face. "I tell you, I didn't take it!" he shouted back. "Sure I liked the cat mummy. Cats fascinate me. That's no secret. But I didn't take it. I saw Vaz take it last night. I thought she was doing research on it so I didn't say anything. Now she claims she didn't do it. Ha!" Vaz and Manx glared at each other.

"That mummified cat was the only one of its kind. I must get it back," Dr. Rogliphic said worriedly, glancing at Hyde and Seek and fumbling in his desk drawer. "Here's a map of the second floor—that's where the Egyptian Room is. I'll mark an X where the cat mummy stood in its display case." He handed the map to Detective Seek.

"Okay," Hyde began, taking out a notepad and pencil. "Let's start at the beginning. Ms. Vaz, did you see Mr. Manx take the mummy?"

Vaz looked down at the floor. "Well, no. I can't say I did. But it was here when I left last night. I do know that!"

Hyde turned to Tom Manx. "When did you see Ms. Vaz take the cat?" he asked.

Manx smirked. "Just after closing time—about 9:10 P.M. I was looking at the ancient mural. It is quite impressive you know. I heard a noise behind me and that's when I saw Vaz put the cat in a bag and take off."

"Are you certain, Mr. Manx?" Seek asked, studying the map. "Is that exactly the way it happened?"

"Exactly!" Manx replied. "No doubt about it."

"Then I'm afraid you've let the cat out of the bag," she continued. "Manx is lying and I can prove it!"

How can she?

Use the Clues

Museums often have maps that show the layout of each floor as well as the location of new exhibits. Dr. Rogliphic handed Detective Seek a map of the museum's second floor. By listening to Manx's story and studying the map, she knew that he was lying. Read Detective Hyde's notes, and then look at the map of the Egyptian Room. Can you catch Manx's lie?

52

Name_____

The Case of the Missing Mummy

DETECTIVE HYDE'S NOTES

Manx says that after closing time (about 9:10 P.M.) he was looking at the ancient mural in the museum's Egyptian Room, which is located on the second floor, when he heard a noise. He claims he turned around and saw Vaz remove the cat mummy from its exhibit case, place the piece in a bag, and then quickly leave the room.

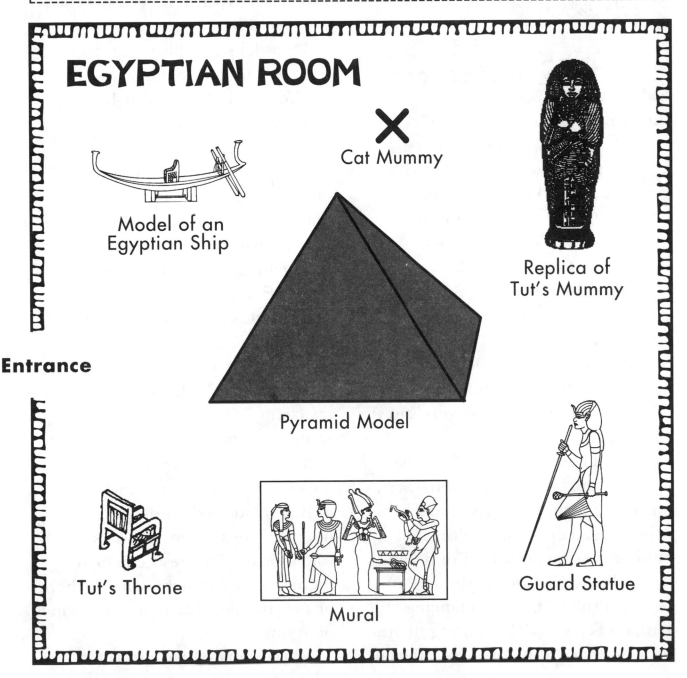

EGYPTIAN ROOM

Model of an Egyptian Ship

✗ Cat Mummy

Replica of Tut's Mummy

Entrance

Pyramid Model

Tut's Throne

Mural

Guard Statue

PURLOINED PITCHER

Or Reading a Weather Map

The Mystery

Butch Buttinski eyed Captain Schwab of the Brown City Police Department. "I was home, I told you. Watching the game. I didn't have anything to do with Johnny Benchwarmer's disappearance! I demand to see my lawyer!"

"I am your lawyer, Mr. Buttinski," a timid voice piped in from the corner.

Butch threw a disgusted look at Marvin Gardens, attorney at law. "You're kind of easy to forget. Know what I mean?"

Marvin cleared his throat. "That may well be, Mr. Buttinski. However, on your behalf, I've hired two private detectives—specialists in the field of missing persons. I'm hoping they'll be able to locate Mr. Benchwarmer," he said, glancing at Captain Schwab. "May I bring them in? They have some questions they'd like to ask Mr. Buttinski."

Captain Schwab nodded as Detectives Hyde and Seek were led into the office.

"Now let's get this straight," Hyde began. "Johnny Benchwarmer, star pitcher of the Brown City baseball team, has been kidnapped, correct?"

"Correct," answered Captain Schwab. "And just before the play-offs with the Palmetto Pests! Benchwarmer's been receiving threatening notes telling him to leave town. He didn't show up for training this morning. We suspect foul play."

Marvin Gardens cleared his throat again. "And, ah, it seems that my client, Mr. Buttinski here, made several comments of a threatening nature to Mr. Benchwarmer during an autograph session last week."

Butch laughed loudly. "So what!" he said. "He's a bum and so's the whole team! The Pests can beat them whether Benchwarmer's there or not. Besides, I have a right to my opinion!"

Marvin turned back to Hyde and

Seek. "And, unfortunately, Mr. Buttinski's handwriting matches that of the threatening notes. And he is known to be a fanatic Palmetto fan. We need to find Mr. Benchwarmer. That's why we've hired you."

Detective Seek glanced at the missing person's report. "It says here that Benchwarmer was last seen leaving batting practice Sunday at 6:00 P.M. Apparently he never even made it to his car in the parking lot. That was yesterday. Where were you at 6:00 that evening?" she asked Butch.

Butch curled his lip. "Watching a baseball game on television at my house. Who's there to say that I wasn't?"

"There was a game on at that time, I can assure you," Marvin said. "Here's a copy of yesterday's television listings." He handed a section of newspaper to Detective Hyde. "See there? Right below the weather report."

Detective Hyde glanced at the paper. "Hmmm, Providence played Little Rock. Who won the game, Mr. Buttinski?"

Butch looked nervous for a moment. "Can't tell you. I fell asleep during the first inning. When I woke up the game was over."

Hyde smiled. "I have a friend who's a sports reporter," he said. "Let me call him and find out who won."

"Who cares who won?!" Captain Schwab exploded as Hyde dialed a number and spoke quietly into the phone. "How is that going to help us find Benchwarmer?"

"Quite easily, Captain," Hyde said, as he hung up the phone. "I suggest you arrest Butch Buttinski for the kidnapping of Johnny Benchwarmer. There was no baseball game last night. Butch is lying!"

How does he know? (Hint: Study the newspaper clipping carefully.)

Use the Clues

A weather map can tell you at a glance what weather to expect in a particular place. The key shows what the symbols used on the map represent; for example, rain, snow, sunshine, even hurricanes. Marvin Gardens handed Detective Hyde a newspaper clipping with television listings and a weather report for Sunday evening. Look at the listings and use the weather map and key to prove that Butch was lying.

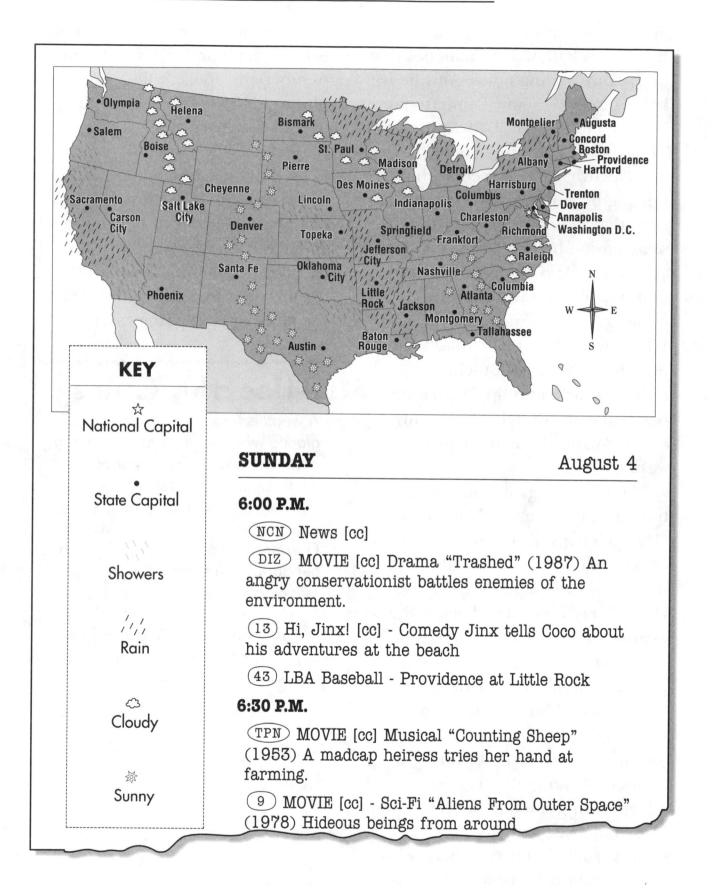

KEY

☆
National Capital

•
State Capital

Showers

Rain

☁
Cloudy

☼
Sunny

SUNDAY   August 4

6:00 P.M.

(NCN) News [cc]

(DIZ) MOVIE [cc] Drama "Trashed" (1987) An angry conservationist battles enemies of the environment.

(13) Hi, Jinx! [cc] - Comedy Jinx tells Coco about his adventures at the beach

(43) LBA Baseball - Providence at Little Rock

6:30 P.M.

(TPN) MOVIE [cc] Musical "Counting Sheep" (1953) A madcap heiress tries her hand at farming.

(9) MOVIE [cc] - Sci-Fi "Aliens From Outer Space" (1978) Hideous beings from around

THE CASE OF THE
DISHONEST ABE
Or Using an Area Code Map

The Mystery

Lydia Fort-Apache was known for her hospitality. "Please, have some more cherry pie and stay a little longer!" she begged, reaching for Detective Hyde's plate. "After all, it's not every day that I get to see my favorite nephew!"

Detective Hyde blushed. "I'm your only nephew, Aunt Lydia," he said.

Lydia laughed. "So you are. Who can keep track of that sort of thing?" She turned toward Detective Seek. "More pie, my dear? I'm so glad you were able to come, as well!"

Detective Seek smiled. "Thank you for inviting me," she said.

Lydia beamed. "I love parties. They're such fun."

A snort came from the corner of the room. "Bah! She'd have a party every day if she could!" Uncle Bronx added sourly.

Aunt Lydia wrinkled her nose

impishly. "Oh, Bronxy—don't be such a sour puss! What will our guests think? After all, it is President's Day . . . . I think! Does anyone have a calendar?"

Detective Hyde smiled and glanced out the window. "It's starting to snow, Aunt Lydia. I think we'd better leave before the roads get slippery. Besides," Hyde added, "all your other guests left hours ago."

"Too true, too true," sighed Aunt Lydia.

Suddenly, a piercing scream followed by a dull thud echoed through the night. "What was that?" Detective Seek gasped.

Uncle Bronx threw on his coat. "I don't know," he said, flipping on the outdoor light. "But it came from outside."

The group hurried through the door. There, heaped on the ground, was a figure dressed like Abraham Lincoln.

"Oh, no!" shouted Aunt Lydia. "He must have fallen off our roof. Is he dead?"

Seek crouched down next to the still body. "No," she answered. "But

57

he might have some broken bones! Let's get him in the house!" Carefully Hyde, Seek, and Uncle Bronx carried the man inside and put him on the sofa.

Lydia looked pale. "It can't be the President. It can't be. Can it?" she mumbled to herself.

Uncle Bronx reached for the telephone. "Of course it isn't, Lydia!" he snapped. "Pull yourself together! I'm calling an ambulance!"

"Better call the police as well!" Hyde said. "This stovepipe hat he was carrying is filled with jewels! This guy's a thief!"

"Jewels!" Aunt Lydia squealed, dumping the contents of the hat on the floor. "Maybe he was bringing them!"

Uncle Bronx picked up several pieces. "Lydia! This is your jewelry!"

"Oh, no!" she pouted. "I thought it looked familiar!"

Minutes later, the police and an ambulance arrived. Officer Blotter of Precinct 43 removed the thief's fake beard. "Looks like you folks have been paid a visit by Doc Holiday!" he said. "We've been looking for this guy for a long time. Every holiday he and his ring of thieves commit a crime. We think they robbed a jewelry store a couple of weeks ago dressed as cupids."

Aunt Lydia cleared her throat. "You said 'ring.' Might there be others still around?" she asked nervously, looking about.

Officer Blotter shook his head. "We got a tip that the rest of the crew fled out of state! I wish we could find them, though!"

Detective Seek handed Officer Blotter a scrap of paper. "Perhaps this will help. We found it in his pocket. It looks like some kind of a list."

Blotter glanced at the paper. "Let's see. . .Bennie (702 Elm Lane), Lennie (602 Ash Bend), Butchie (503 Oak Cove), and Sam (801 Fir Road). Sounds like them, all right! Let me get back to headquarters. We'll get a statement from you folks later!"

Several hours went by before Officer Blotter returned. "How's the president?" Aunt Lydia asked worriedly.

"A broken arm, but he'll be okay," Blotter answered. "If only we could get him to talk about where the rest of the thieves are."

Uncle Bronx raised an eyebrow. "But I thought you chaps had that address list."

Officer Blotter scratched his head. "We checked those addresses—all fake! We showed it to Doc but he claims that it's his birthday card list!"

Detective Hyde glanced at Detective Seek. "May we look at that list again, Officer?" he asked as he headed for the phone. "Aunt Lydia, can you find the telephone book?"

Officer Blotter looked puzzled. "Here's the list," he said, handing Seek the paper. "What are you two getting at? We've already checked those addresses!"

Detective Hyde smiled. "Those aren't addresses. They're telephone numbers," he explained. "Give us a few minutes and I'll tell you what states the thieves are in and their phone numbers. They're just a phone call away!"

Officer Blotter looked puzzled. "I don't understand!"

Do you?

The Case of the Dishonest Abe

DOC HOLIDAY'S LIST

Bennie:
702 Elm Lane

Lennie:
602 Ash Bend

Butchie:
503 Oak Cove

Sam:
801 Fir Road

Use the Clues

Detective Hyde asked for Doc Holiday's list and a telephone book and then he went to the phone. Why? A telephone number is made up of 10 digits—a three-digit area code (which tells you what state or what part of the state a number is in), followed by three digits (known as the exchange), a hyphen, and then four more digits. An area code map, located in the front of most telephone books, can help you find the area code for a particular place. The letters of the alphabet (except Q and Z) are printed on a telephone dial or touch pad. Each letter corresponds to a number (except 0 and 1). Use Doc Holiday's list, the telephone touch pad, and the area code map to find the location and telephone number of each thief.

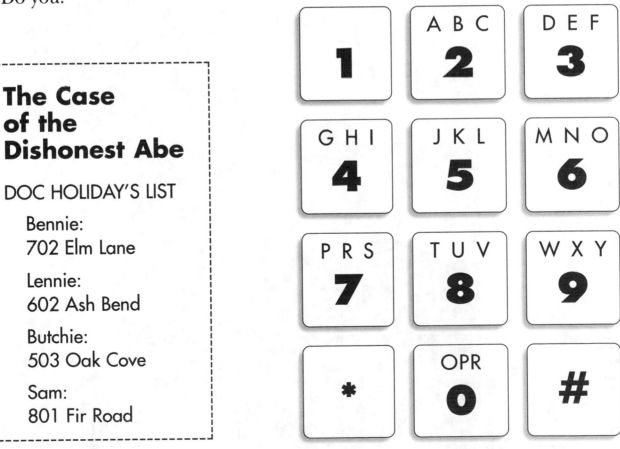

Area Code Map

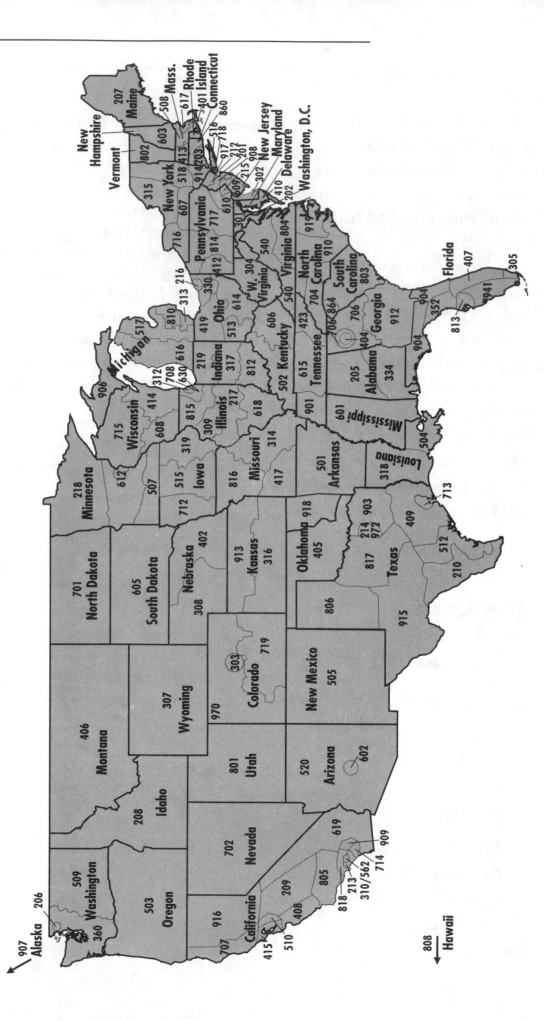

THE CASE OF THE
DISAPPEARING DIPLOMAT
Or Using a Marine Chart

The Mystery

Detective Hyde enjoyed visiting his uncle at the shore for the weekend. Captain Andy Hyde lived in a tiny house next to the gorgeous lawns and huge beach-front home of Ambassador Terrain of Gwanelia. Seated with his nephew and Detective Seek in a small skiff, the May B. Knott, he called their attention to the ambassador's house. "The ambassador is giving a fancy party for all his wealthy friends tonight!" he chuckled. "Neighborhood's really changed. Used to be just a small fishing village."

The Captain turned to Detective Seek. "I used to be an oyster man in these parts," he explained, as he took them around Montapeake Point. "Today most of the oystering is done commercially. See that?" he asked, pointing to the top of a mast sticking out of the water near the beach. "It's the wreck of the Will B. Able—one of the best oyster boats around. I remember when we lost her in the storm of '62." The boat headed around the peninsula and past an old lighthouse. Captain Andy smiled. "There's Montapeake Point lighthouse! My best friend Abe Tarr was the keeper. But those days are long gone." Suddenly he shouted to his nephew, "Sonny, look out for Blackperch Rock!"

Hyde expertly took the boat away from a large, dark shape under the surface of the water. "That rock scares the life out of me!" he sighed.

As the sun began to set the trio returned to Captain Andy's house for a hearty Friday night dinner of oyster chowder. Sounds of music and gay laughter from the the ambassador's mansion filled the evening air. The noise continued long after Captain Andy, Hyde, and Seek snuggled into three hammocks strung up in the small living room.

Early Saturday morning, they were awakened by a new sound—a panicked knocking at the front door. "Who could that be at this hour?" Captain Andy said, as they all struggled out of their hammocks.

They opened the door to find Ambassador Terrain nervously wringing his hands. "Sorry to wake you," he began hurriedly, "but this is an emergency. Have you seen the Carmelitian Ambassador, Errada Cubota?" The trio at the door shook their heads. The ambassador turned pale. "I'm afraid he's missing! He went out for a walk on the beach last night and never returned."

Captain Andy grew alarmed. "Better call the police," he said wisely. "And maybe two of us could search the beach…." His words were interrupted by the sight of a bedraggled man stumbling up the road.

"Ambassador Cubota!" shouted Ambassador Terrain. The group helped Cubota into Captain Andy's house and into a chair.

"What happened?" Detective Seek asked.

Ambassador Cubota wiped his face with a handkerchief. "I was kidnapped!" he gasped. "I was walking along the beach near the old shipwreck at about 2:00 in the morning. Suddenly two men blindfolded me and put me in a small boat. They tied me up and left me on a rock all night!" Noticing a large marine chart on the captain's wall he pointed to it. "There's the shipwreck I was looking at. And there's the rock they left me on— Blackperch Rock! They planned on coming back for me at daybreak with a larger vessel. Fortunately, I managed to break the ropes tying me up and wade back to shore!" He indicated the bottoms of his pants which were soaked with water.

Ambassador Terrain looked concerned. "Poor man! Do you have any idea who did this?" he asked.

Cubota narrowed his eyes. "I have no doubt. The men had Cocoan accents!"

Ambassador Terrain gasped. Everyone knew that the countries of Carmelita and Cocoa did not get along. "This may mean war!" shouted Cubota.

Detective Hyde studied the marine chart carefully. "Did you say you were on Blackperch Rock all night?" he asked.

Cubota looked annoyed. "Of course!" he shouted angrily. "Are you doubting my word?"

Hyde glanced at the tide schedule posted near the chart. "I'm sorry Ambassador, but according to the tide schedule and the marine chart, you're not telling the truth!"

How does he know?

Use the Clues

After looking at both the marine chart and the tide schedule, Detective Hyde said he could tell that Ambassador Cubota was lying. How? A marine chart is a special type of map. It helps boaters navigate, or travel, a body of water in safety. A marine chart usually shows coastlines, harbors, lighthouses, and buoys as well as the depth of the water in different places. (That's what the numbers scattered on the map refer to.) Knowing the water depth can help alert boaters to possible hazards such as rocks or old ship wrecks. Most marine charts show how deep the water is at low tide. A certain spot that is 2 feet deep at low tide might be 4 feet deep at high tide. Why? A tide is the movement of water that comes over the shore (high tide) and then goes out again (low tide). A tide schedule tells whether the tide is high or low. Now look at the marine chart of Montapeake Point and Montapeake Bay and find Blackperch Rock. Then look at the schedule of tides for Friday and Saturday. Can you prove that Ambassador Cubota was lying?

TIDE SCHEDULE FOR MONTAPEAKE BAY
Eastern Daylight Time (EDT)

Day	HH:MM	Feet	HH:MM	Feet	HH:MM	Feet	HH:MM	Feet
Friday	00:39 A.M.	3.6	06:52 A.M.	-1.1	01:09 P.M.	3.5	07:48 P.M.	0.2
Saturday	02:03 A.M.	4.0	08:30 A.M.	-1.0	02:58 P.M.	3.0	09:10 P.M.	1.1

(- = low tide)

Marine Chart

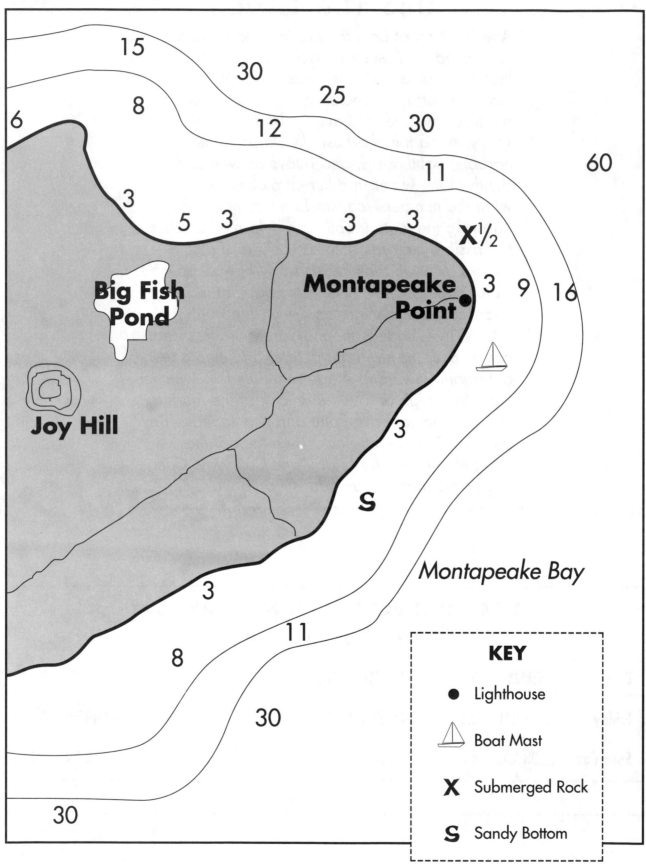

15

30

8

25

6

12

30

3

60

5　3

11

3　3

X½

Big Fish Pond

Montapeake Point ●

3　9　16

3

Joy Hill

3

S

Montapeake Bay

3

11

8

30

KEY

● Lighthouse

⛵ Boat Mast

X Submerged Rock

S Sandy Bottom

30

THE SOLUTIONS

THE CASE OF THE PUZZLING PRODUCER
Or Identifying Geographic Shapes

Uncle J.D. did know his kidnapper! He removed those puzzle pieces that would spell out his kidnapper's name. The missing pieces of the puzzle are the states of Idaho, California, Louisiana, Kentucky, and Florida. By rearranging the first letter of each state, Hyde came up with the name Flick. When he knew that he was trapped, Flick admitted to having kidnapped his uncle for the ransom money. J.D. was found unharmed, locked up in Flick's mountain cabin. ***Case solved!***

THE CASE OF THE BORDERLINE FANATIC
Or Interpreting Map Borderlines

Hyde noticed that the birds crossed from state to state, from county to county, and finally from country to country. By checking the map key, he identified the following boundary line symbols:
– . – . state, – – – county, and
– . . – international (between different countries). By looking up the Morse code letter for each set of symbols, Hyde was able to figure out that Cox, J. Hilary Cox, was going to be the next victim. With close surveillance, the police were able to catch the kidnappers red-handed. ***Case solved!***

THE CASE OF THE PINCHED POOCHES
Or Identifying Continents and Capital Cities

After pinpointing the place where each dog was stolen, Detective Hyde noticed a pattern. Each animal was taken from the capital city of one of the countries located on five of the seven continents. Two continents remained—Antarctica and Australia. Because Antarctica has no capital city, Hyde figured that the next dog would have to be taken from Canberra, the capital of Australia. By posting undercover police officers around Bob, the silky terrier belonging to the prime minister of Australia, Mr. Pregoria was able to catch the kidnappers red-handed. The other dogs were found unharmed and returned to their grateful owners. ***Case solved!***

THE CASE OF THE ABBREVIATED ARTIST
Or Identifying Map Abbreviations

After deciphering the abbreviations, Juan Palazzo was able to reach Pablo Paletto and confirm that his painting was authentic. ***Case solved!***
1. Mountain
2. North Carolina
3. Highway
4. Parkway
5. Street
6. River

7. Road
8. Lane
9. Cove
10. Point
11. Lake
12. Island

THE CASE OF THE ABSENT ARCHEOLOGIST
Or Using a Compass Rose

Starting at the City in the Mist, Detective Hyde traced a line south by southwest to Snake River, west by northwest to Murky Lake high in the mountains, north by northeast to Beasty Mountain, and east by southeast back to the City in the Mist. By connecting each point and drawing intersecting lines, Hyde saw just where to go. Three days later Dr. Stone was found in the Valley of Darkness, happily uncovering shimmering objects made of rubies, diamonds, and sapphires. *Case solved!*

THE CASE OF THE VANISHING SISTERS
Or Using a Grid Map

The bingo hall was really controlled by a gang of busy international art thieves. Information on where stolen artifacts were hidden was given out on specially-marked bingo cards. The bingo caller would identify the location of stolen art by using the coordinates of the city map. By using the winning bingo numbers as coordinates, Detective Seek helped locate the statues at the following locations:

B3 Jon's Sports Store;
I8 Harry's Restaurant;
N2 Mitzi's Pizzeria;
G5 The Amazing Video Store; and
O7 The Cloak and Dagger Book Store.
The statues were returned to the museum in Italy.
Case solved!

THE CASE OF THE MISSING MILLIONAIRES
Or Determining Latitude and Longitude

Armed with the map, Detective Seek used her finger to trace the 18° S latitude line until it touched the 178° E longitude line. The island of Fiji is located at the point where the two lines cross. The Lottabucks were picked up the next day pulling into the Port of Suva on Fiji. *Case solved!*

THE CASE OF THE ELVIS IMPERSONATOR
Or Using a Map Scale

Roncoco said he filled up his gas tank in St. Louis. You remember that his car has a 20-gallon tank and gets about 10 miles per gallon. That means Roncoco could go 200 miles without stopping for more gasoline (20 X 10). By using the map scale, Detective Seek figured that the distance from St. Louis to Memphis was about 260 miles. Roncoco could never have made it from St. Louis to Memphis on just one tank of gasoline. When faced with the facts, Roncoco confessed to stopping in Cape Girardeau and robbing the gas station there. *Case solved!*

THE CASE OF THE SMILING SEÑORITA
Or Comparing Time Zones

Fey claimed that he was in New York City watching the live broadcast of the royal wedding. However, the royal wedding was at 12:00 noon in *London*. By looking at the time zone map, Detective Seek showed that when it is 12:00 noon in London, it is 7 A.M. in New York City. So, the wedding was long over in New York at the time Fey insisted that he was watching. When confronted with this fact, Fey admitted that he had been in London for the royal wedding and had indeed stolen the painting of the Smiling Señorita from the Duke of Worcestershire's home. The painting was soon recovered. *Case solved!*

THE CASE OF THE MISSING MONSTER
Or Reading a Contour Map

By looking at the contour map, Hyde and Seek saw that Lord Hugo was camped at the top of Mount Monstrosity. In his description, he states that he heard a noise as the sun was rising. When he confronted the hairy creature, Hugo claims it took off, running downhill straight into the rising sun. Now remember that the sun rises in the east. By looking at the map, Hyde and Seek saw that the east side of Mount Monstrosity is drawn with contour lines extremely close together—indicating a very steep cliff. Anyone running directly east would have fallen off the mountain. When faced with these facts, Hugo admitted to having made up the story about the abominable snowman in order to get publicity for his next mountain climbing trip. *Case solved!*

THE CASE OF THE RANSOMED ROCKER
Or Using a Street Map

Seek carefully traced Pic's route on the street map. She marked where he first signed his autograph with his left hand outside of Tune's Guitars. She next marked where the phony Pic signed his name with his right hand—outside of Twisted Scissors. Since Pic was in sight the entire time from Tune's Guitars to Twisted Scissors, he must have disappeared at the hair salon. When questioned by the police, Tisa Shears, the owner of the salon, admitted to kidnapping Pic and dressing in his clothes to throw anyone suspicious off the trail. When the fake Pic went into Java Joe's, she changed back into her own clothes and left the restaurant. Pic was later found unharmed, locked up in the basement of the salon. *Case solved!*

THE CASE OF THE MISSING MICROCHIP
Or Reading a Road Map

The hideout was located just north of Riverdale on an unpaved road. The thieves were still outside when Dexter and Hata arrived to retrieve the valuable microchip from the closet where it had been hidden. *Case solved!*

THE CASE OF THE SNATCHED SCIENTIST
Or Reading a Resource Map

Detective Hyde knew from the clues that the kidnappers had called from an area that caught and sold seafood (an oyster knife for shelling oysters and paper used to wrap fish). He also knew that Fermenti was being held in a factory. By using the resource map, he and Detective Seek found a factory located in an area rich with fish and oysters. Investigators soon found Professor Fermenti and his kidnappers at the Half-Shell Seafood Factory in Bunsville. *Case solved!*

THE CASE OF THE BAGGED BERTHA
Or Using a Zoo Map

Each of the boys had an alibi, or claim that he was somewhere else when the tarantula was stolen. Spider took Harry to the first aid station—a call to the nurse-on-duty proved that. Chuck and Bart claimed to have walked to the Aviary for the 10:00 show. Since everyone left the Insect/Spider House at 10:00, it's believable that they would have missed the first ten minutes of the show. The other boys claimed to have taken the tram when it arrived at stop #2 that would have been at 10:10. Milton said he got off at stop #4 for the feeding of the big cats. The tram would have arrived at stop #4 at 10:30. Since the lions weren't being fed until 10:35, Milton would have had time to see the feeding. Hugo claims he got off at stop #5 for the monkey show. However, the show started at 10:00 and ended at 10:30. Hugo's tram wouldn't have arrived at stop #5 until 10:40. Hugo would have missed the show! When confronted, Hugo admitted to taking Big Bertha out of her cage and hiding her in his pocket. He actually rode the tram to stop #7 and walked to the picnic area, where he put Big Bertha in his lunch bag. Aside from being covered with peanut-butter sandwich crumbs, Bertha was returned to her cage unharmed. *Case solved!*

THE CASE OF THE MISSING MUMMY
Or Interpreting a Museum Map

An X marks the spot where the mummified cat stood. Tom Manx says he saw Ming Vaz take the cat when he was looking at the ancient mural. But he couldn't have seen anyone take the cat because the 30-foot model of the Great Pyramid would have blocked his sight. When confronted with this fact, Manx admitted to have taken the mummified cat to add to his collection. *Case solved!*

THE CASE OF THE PURLOINED PITCHER
Or Reading a Weather Map

By looking at the television listings, Detective Hyde saw that Little Rock was supposed to play Providence at home. By looking at the weather map, he also saw that heavy rain was expected in Little Rock. Baseball games are usually canceled when the weather is bad. When Hyde called his friend, the sports reporter, he was able to prove that the game had been rained out that night. Caught in a lie,

Butch admitted to having locked Johnny Benchwarmer in his storage shed. *Case solved!*

THE CASE OF THE DISHONEST ABE
Or Using an Area Code Map

By finding the number on the telephone touch pad that corresponds to each letter of the address, Detectives Hyde and Seek were quickly able to come up with a list for Officer Blotter. Remember, the street number represents the area code.

Bennie: (702) 356-5263 (Nevada)
Lennie: (602) 274-2363 (Arizona)
Butchie: (503) 625-2683 (Oregon)
Sam: (801) 347-7623 (Utah)

The telephone numbers were traced and the thieves were all rounded up. *Case solved!*

THE CASE OF THE DISAPPEARING DIPLOMAT
Or Using a Marine Chart

By looking at the tide schedule, Detective Hyde saw that high tide came in at 2:03 A.M. and went out at 8:30 A.M. According to the marine chart, not only is Blackperch Rock under water, it's under $4\frac{1}{2}$ feet of water at high tide! If the ambassador had been on Blackperch Rock all night more than just the bottom of his pants would have been wet! When confronted with the truth, Ambassador Cubota admitted to trying to start trouble with the ambassador from Cocoa. *Case solved!*

Notes

Notes